Christ Returns to the Soviets

REVOLUTION OF THE HEART

Greg Gulley and Kim Parker

HUNTINGTON HOUSE PUBLISHERS

Huntington House Publishers
P.O. Box 53788
Lafayette, Louisiana 70505

Library of Congress Card Catalog Number
93-77300
ISBN 1-56384-041-3

Scripture quotations are from the following:

The Amplified Bible

*The New American Standard Bible Reference
Edition*

The Holy Bible New Internatonal Version

CONTENTS

1

But you will receive power when the Holy Spirit comes on you; and you will be my witnesses in Jerusalem, and in all Judea and Samaria, and to the ends of the earth.

(Acts 1:8)

1

Our Upper Room

"Who? Greg Gulley?"

That's my name, I thought as I rounded the corner on the second flight of stairs in our Helsinki hotel and faced a bewildered receptionist talking on the phone. The timing was perfect. "I'm Greg Gulley," I answered. With a confused glance, she handed me the receiver. "Greg," Gary said, "I'm sorry, but I have some bad news. The Soviet contact called, and your visas have been denied."

My heart sank. We had not been in Helsinki two hours when we received this devastating news from our home office in Raleigh, North Carolina. In a moment, I saw evaporating the work, prayers, and labors of one full year of preparation.

Communication to the Soviet Union was impossible during much of the preparation. We seriously considered sending someone from our office to do the advance work for this trip. Finally, phone contact was made and the problems seemed to clear. Rhoni Hammond and others at the Youth With A Mission (YWAM) offices in Oregon helped us nail down the invitations and settle the equipment problems. Their help was invaluable in initiating contact with our Soviet sponsors. The team was primed. YWAM Slavic Ministries' Shane Murray told us that we were blazing pioneer territory on the heels of a new openness.

Before leaving the New Life Ministries office that

July morning bound for Raleigh airport, we met for a
final time of prayer and reflection. I shared again with
the group my belief that God was calling us to gird
ourselves about like Jesus (John 13:2-5) and to ready
our hearts to be His servants, willing to wash each
other's feet, and particularly willing to wash the feet of
those to whom God had called us to minister—the
children of the Soviet Union. Any thought of our own
comfort had to take a back seat to the purpose of
Christ.

I again encouraged them to embrace our mission.
With eleven surrendered individuals, God could accomplish extraordinary things. We knew that we stood at
a fragile time and place in history. A glimmer of light
had appeared shining through a door that had been
barred and chained for seven decades. We had to be
poised to seize this "once in a lifetime" opportunity. It
demanded that we stay on the edge of our seats spiritually.

Landing in Helsinki, Finland, we knew that our
vision, prayers, and dreams were only a day from fruition. Then the news came from our office. Little did I
know just how much our team would be tested before
we saw the fruit of God's plan.

As I hung up the phone with Gary, questions raced
through my mind. I now knew what people meant when
they referred to that "sinking feeling." It is as if your
heart numbs and deflates simultaneously. We were
halfway across the world, did not speak the language,
and our return tickets were useless for weeks. My own
return was to be in another ten days, and the team's
tickets were for returning from East Germany, where
they were scheduled to travel after the Soviet Union.
What were we going to do?

Gathering the team together, I made the announcement. As I surveyed the ten faces before me, I could see
the rise of a determination that seemed to acknowl-
edge that our battle was not of flesh and blood, but a
battle to be fought strategically in the heavenlies. We
organized. One person went to speak first with a travel

agent in Finland who was arranging the visas and then to the Soviet Embassy. Another team member and I journeyed the one-mile trek to the post office to make some phone calls. Our hotel rooms had no telephones. The remainder of the team began immediately to intercede, undergirding our efforts and beginning the necessary movements in the heavenlies.

I immediately called the YWAM base. They too began interceding in our behalf and faxing messages to the Soviet Union around the clock. I called my wife, Lynn, to alert her that she would serve as a catalyst for communication with YWAM and our Soviet contacts if they could not get through to us in Helsinki. Reports came back from our initial inquiries that our visas were denied because our invitation did not come from a recognized firm. Officials at the Soviet Embassy informed us that initiating another invitation and securing legitimate visas would take at least ten days with no guarantee of success.

As we did everything we knew to do logistically, I was reminded that this trip, twelve months in the planning, was completely guided by the Lord. There was every reason to believe, even in the midst of seemingly impossible obstacles, that He would see us through to complete victory. Our task was to persevere, diligently and seriously seeking His face.

The Holy Spirit prompted me to review His signposts along the way. He reminded me of my first meeting with Jim Dikih of YWAM's Slavic Ministries. It was in August 1989, that Jim visited our church as a last minute speaker to share the heart-rending occurrences of recent days in the Soviet Union. We had been performing our children's musical, *The Greatest Star of All*, for over two years and *Never Be the Same* for one in cities across the United States.

I always envisioned that the musicals' circus setting would lend to their acceptance abroad. Clowns, a lion, a tiger, and a bear could cross cultural and even language barriers. Our focus prior to my introduction to Jim, however, was reaching the children of this nation. We were praying about opportunities abroad but not actively pursuing any.

As I approached Jim after the service to thank him for coming and to offer my family's support in his efforts, a friend shouted, "Jim, these guys have a dynamic children's ministry!" He responded with enthusiasm and explained that ministries in the Soviet Union and Eastern Europe needed to concentrate on the future generations. In fact, children's outreach was the most critical need, children having been the most guarded possessions of the Soviet regime.

We talked for a few minutes, and I shared with him about our ministry. That conversation began the year-long process of preparing for our first outreaches abroad—in the Soviet Union.

God also reminded me now of how He divinely engineered our attendance at a training session on the YWAM Slavic Ministries base in Salem, Oregon. The Red Team's first tour of 1990 was on the West coast. When they left, our trip abroad was in the initial planning stages. Adjusting their schedule to accommodate training and orientation for the trip seemed impossible. With the collapse of the Berlin Wall, YWAM was inundated with requests for overseas training. In order to handle this large number of inquiries, they departed from their normal procedure of sending staff out in the field and scheduled one large training session at the base in Oregon. As God would have it, the Red Team was in Oregon the week that this training was scheduled and had several days off that coincided with the session—the only days open on a packed two-month tour.

During my flight to meet the team, the Lord gave me two passages of Scripture that proved to be pillars of truth and promise for our trip. The first was Joshua 1:2-9:

> Moses my servant is dead; now therefore arise, cross the Jordan, you and all these people, to the land which I am giving to them, to the sons of Israel. Every place on which the sole of your foot

treads, I have given it to you, just as I spoke to Moses. From the wilderness and this Lebanon, even as far as the great river, the river Euphrates, all the land of the Hittites, and as far as the Great Sea toward the setting of the sun, will be your territory. No man will be able to stand before you all the days of your life. Just as I have been with Moses, I will be with you; I will not fail you nor forsake you. Be strong and courageous, for you shall give this people possession of the land which I swore to their fathers to give them. Only be strong and very courageous; be careful to do according to all the law which Moses My servant commanded you; do not turn from it to the right or to the left, so that you may have success wherever you go. This book of the law shall not depart from your mouth, but you shall meditate on it day and night, so that you may be careful to do according to all that is written in it; for then you will make your way prosperous, and then you will have success. Have I not commanded you? Be strong and courageous! Do not tremble or be dismayed, for the Lord your God is with you wherever you go.

The second, Jeremiah 1:4-10:

Now the word of the Lord came to me saying, "Before I formed you in the womb I knew you, and before you were born I consecrated you; I have appointed you a prophet to the nations." Then I said, "Alas, Lord God! Behold, I do not know how to speak, because I am a youth." But the Lord said to me, "Do not say, I am a youth, because everywhere I send you, you shall go, and all that I command you, you shall speak. Do not be afraid of them, for I am with you to deliver you," declares the Lord. Then the Lord stretched out his hand and touched my mouth, and the Lord said to me, "Behold, I have put my words in your mouth. See, I have appointed you this day over the nations and the kingdoms, to pluck up and to break down, to destroy and to overthrow, to build and to plant."

During our stay at the YWAM base, we had intercession with the team. In that time, the Lord gave us additional promises that overwhelmed us with their correlation to Scriptures He had already laid on our hearts. Isaiah 45:2-3 was shared, and we were struck by its significance. It reads: "I will go before you and make the rough places smooth; I will shatter the gates of bronze, and cut through the iron bars. And I will give you the treasures of darkness, and hidden wealth in secret places, in order that you may know that it is I, the Lord, the God of Israel, who calls you by name."

In the days before our departure, we lived on those promises. Each day, a different phrase brought new purpose and strength.

Now in the midst of this crisis in Helsinki that threatened the entire trip, God sent me running back to those verses and to the plans that demonstrated His sovereign hand. He had indeed orchestrated the events up to this point, and He would see us through this struggle as well. My prayer: "What do you require of us now, Lord?" We were willing to do whatever He asked.

That evening we all gathered to seek Him and avail ourselves in spiritual battle. Helsinki was to become our upper room. It was clear that nothing short of a miracle from God would result in our setting foot on Soviet soil. I knew that the team could have easily had their doubts. They were not as intimately involved in the events that brought us to Helsinki, and our circumstances appeared grim. In the natural, we were completely hemmed in with nowhere to go. They knew that we were breaking new ground, and I am certain they felt like lonely pioneers in our Helsinki wilderness.

The Lord led me to 2 Chronicles 20 and to Acts 16. Comparable to the events that faced Jehosophat and the people of God, we confronted overwhelming odds with no natural recourse. In the face of those obstacles, the Lord said to Jehosophat, "Do not be afraid or discouraged because of this vast army. For the battle is not yours, but God's . . . You will not have to fight this battle. Take up your positions; stand firm and see the deliverance the Lord will give you." In obedience, Jehosophat appointed men to sing praises to the Lord, leading the army into battle. As they lifted their voices in worship, Scripture tells us that God caused each of the three opposing armies to set ambushes for each other. The army of Jehosophat never lifted a sword. Worship was the only weapon employed by the Lord's army. For three days they collected the spoils of victory.

The team could take comfort that this struggle was not ours but the Lord's. We were not alone. After all, the mission before us belonged to Him. As we prayed for direction, we all sensed that we were to do intense spiritual battle in prayer and worship. Just as Paul and Silas were bound in chains in the inner prison in Acts 16, we too were imprisoned by our circumstances. We needed God to break not only the chains that prevented us from entering the Soviet Union but also those chains that held the people's hearts as well. We prayed that God would shake the very foundations of the Soviet government and the people and give us favor with the Soviet officials handling our visas.

In the face of impossible circumstances, Paul and Silas looked unto God with eyes of faith. In the midst of those circumstances, they did spiritual battle, worshiping and praising Him until the midnight hour. At the dark hour of midnight, God thrust His sovereign hand into the inner prison and shook its foundation, breaking the chains that bound Paul and Silas.

This was indeed our midnight hour—the dark hour when our circumstances seemed to be on the verge of engulfing the labor of an entire year. In intercession at YWAM, the staff saw the Strongman with his arms crossed standing between Helsinki and the Soviet Union.

We easily ignored the busy street below and the sound of music from a nearby Finnish night spot as the sweet sounds of worship filled the air of our hotel room and ascended to God's throne. His Presence makes any foreign, strange land seem like home. Although it was 9:00 P.M. and we had been in prayer and worship for two hours, I felt God's leading us to follow the example

of Paul and Silas, worshiping through the midnight
hour. This time proved rich as we sought to be faithful
to His mission. The team members' hearts were visibly
breaking as we waged battle. As we confronted an
obstacle that robbed us of time in the Soviet Union, the
desire to break our chains and minister to this lost
nation intensified. We began to understand and iden-
tify with the bondage of the Soviet people.

At the conclusion of our worship, we knew God had
broken through in the spiritual realm. His assurance
and peace, coupled with a strength of courage, filled
our hearts to overflowing. He had defeated the
Strongman. It was only a matter of time before we
would see His victory manifested in the natural.

The next morning we trusted God to unfold deeper
vision. Reading through Philippians, we sensed His
calling us to a concentrated time of intercession. We
formed a prayer chain, dividing into pairs with each
duo praying for an hour and sharing what they learned
with the two scheduled to relieve them.

During this time, God confirmed His priorities. He
wanted to break our hearts for the children; to get our
minds off physical comforts that could inhibit our mission; to give us a vision that, as we ministered unto the
least of these children, we were ministering unto Jesus;
and to teach us total reliance and dependence upon
Him and His plans. Helsinki was indeed to be our
upper room where we waited for and trusted Him to
empower us to be His witnesses—our upper room where
we saw again His body broken for the world, His life
blood spilled for the lost sheep. Yes, it was an upper
room filled with the communion of His presence and
the indelible impression of His purpose for our lives.

Although our scheduled hours in Helsinki turned
into three days, God redeemed the time as we fought in
prayer and worship, learning to lay our lives before
Him as surrendered vessels. The team responded to all
that was required of them. The cultural differences
posed little distraction. When we were not together in

prayer, worship or study, I found them individually reading and studying the Word. It was a delight to lead such faithful warriors. God taught us important principles of preparation during this time. We could clearly see the vision of God and embark upon His mission, but if we had not come to the place where we relinquished our will to His timing and His plan, then our efforts would have proved unproductive and ineffective.

I treasured that time in Helsinki as a wonderful place of total reliance on God—a wilderness of sorts. Physically separated from all that was familiar, we were not distracted from hearing the Lord speak. The wilderness should never be despised. The Holy Spirit led Jesus into the wilderness, and the Spirit would never misdirect the Son of God. For Jesus, it was a place of transition and preparation. Helsinki was our wilderness of transition and preparation. Whenever a farmer plows new ground, he first must clear the land of trees. Then he must bulldoze the undergrowth. Finally, every stump and root below the ground must be pulled and discarded. Only after a period of intense preparation is the land ready for cultivation as the first seed is sown.

God is a God of preparation, and He is more interested in a deep work than a quick work. We cannot just "show up" to minister and expect God to move in and through us. It is necessary that God deeply prepare the vessels, the hearts and lives of those surrendered under His loving hand. In Helsinki, God taught us those principles that would sustain us throughout the entire trip and lay the pattern for future endeavors.

On the third day, I got through to the Soviet Union and was informed that a new invitation had been issued—a virtual impossibility as the bureaucracy of the U.S.S.R. is known for its red tape and delays. God resurrected our trip. We could pick up our visas the next day and ferry across the Gulf of Finland to Estonia.

Almighty God fought for us. It was His battle, and we emerged victorious only because He fought on our behalf. While we were obedient in prayer and worship, God reminded our Soviet contact that he knew the deputy director of the Latvian State Youth Theater. He enlisted the help of this gentleman, Sergei Shendrick, who generated an invitation from the Youth Theater and filed it with the Soviet Ministry of Foreign Affairs. It was then telexed to the Soviet Embassy in Helsinki.

Our initial visas were to come from a private company. The visas God provided were issued by the Soviet government. Consequently, we became the first Christian touring group in over seventy years to enter the country by government invitation. We witnessed God use an obstacle meant for the disaster of our mission to place us in the strongest of positions. We serve a mighty God! It was time for celebration!

That night we experienced an incredible time of worship, followed by communion. Each team member wept as he meditated upon Jesus' great sacrifice for our sins. The seriousness of our mission inspired each of us anew. God demonstrated that He was much more serious about His work than we could ever be. He answered our prayers in miraculous ways, breaking our hearts for the children as they had never been broken. Only through broken vessels can His love pour. God's ways are not our ways!

2

Every place on which the sole of your foot treads, I have given it to you.

(Josh. 1:3)

Entering Our Promised Land

The four-hour ferry ride across the Sea of Finland to Tallinn, Estonia, was a restful time for the team. The weather was beautiful and the seas calm. It was a time of refreshment and physical renewal that only God can give. We left the Helsinki port arrayed with a sea of sailing yachts lining the harbor, canvases harnessing the warm summer breeze. The water glistened, reflecting a modern skyline and row upon row of costly office buildings and apartments. Canvas window awnings lit the blue sky in a celebration of color. Rich aromas filled the air as street vendors readied sumptuous meals for the many tourists ambling along the picturesque streets. All these scenes soon gave way to another world. The difference was both startling and saddening.

With my first glimpse of Estonia, I was struck with the incredible irony of our situation. The air of freedom on the ferry as we approached the Soviet Union was such a stark contrast to all that we grew up learning about this nation. We were raised to harbor nothing but animosity for an oppressive Soviet regime. Growing up in the sixties meant being subjected to the iciest hatreds and mistrusts of the Cold War. The image of Khrushchev defiantly banging his shoe at the United Nations, promising to bury every American man, woman, and child, was etched in my memory. The frenzy to build fallout shelters made an indelible im-

pression. Civil defense practice prepared school children for a nuclear attack. At the signals, whole classrooms crouched under their desks one by one. These
childhood memories were vivid for me. The Soviet Union
had always been the Evil Empire!

Standing on the deck of the ferry, straining to make
out every detail, we gazed, not upon the Evil Empire,
but upon our promised land. The desire to set foot on
Soviet soil could not have consumed our hearts any
more than it did at that moment.

We docked in a bay and disembarked, negotiating
our equipment down a long stairway. It was about
10:00 P.M., but the sun was just setting since we were
so close to the Arctic Circle. Just as we imagined, the
first face we saw was that of a Soviet soldier. They
were stationed about every twenty feet along the walk
into customs.

Tallinn is the capital of Estonia. It is an old port
city with countless manufacturing plants. The land
terraced away from us as we approached the bay, and
we could see for miles, every now and again catching a
glimpse of an old church—remnants of a forsaken history. The horror stories of Soviet customs raced through
our minds as we walked into the damp, dimly lit building. We prayed as we walked up to the uniformed
officials in shadowed booths.

The team leader passed through the line last with
all the equipment. Expecting to be held up for some
time with questions and searches, we prayed intensely
as Scott approached the booth. At that moment, a Soviet official to whom Scott had given some bananas
only moments earlier emerged from the booth and
waved us through, without ever glancing at our twenty-
eight pieces of equipment. Again, God's unseen hand
guided His servants through yet another obstacle; a
Red Sea parted.

Two Russians, a young man and woman who both
looked to be in their middle thirties, eyed us. Their
expressions indicated that they recognized our green
Greatest Star of All T-shirts. Otis, our bus driver, spoke

no English, and Sveta, our hostess for the trip to Latvia, spoke very little and was obviously nervous about sharing her second language with the first Americans she had ever encountered. We exchanged limited greetings and departed the port to embark upon our four-hour bus trip to Latvia. Night had fallen, so our first impression of life beyond customs was no impression at all. Sveta brought Pepsi, bread, fruit, smoked pork, and beef for us. We did not know at the time what a sacrifice she made in bringing us those meager rations. The average Soviet salary at that time was under 300 rubles a month.

Attempting to set our nervous hostess at ease, we sang American worship songs for her and stumbled through conversation. She had such a sweet spirit but was very open about possessing no relationship with Christ. She observed our worship intently, and I studied her tearful eyes as if to grasp some insight into what this sweet woman had endured. Our early morning concert was more spontaneous than beautiful, but Sveta sat entranced nonetheless by our meager offering in song.

Sveta was our first glimpse of this vast nation's people. I could not help but wonder if we would be able to relate to a people who had endured such hardship. Not only did they have a history of deceit and oppression, but that legacy still plagued their present existence. The society was beginning to open; our presence was evidence of that. Yet the people were no better off. Fear had become a habit, one that they could not shake. The Soviet government was crumbling; the economy was in a state of collapse. Impending doom was a part of everyday existence.

In our research prior to the trip, we read and saw pictures of the endless food lines formed outside stores with bare shelves. We read of the ruble's plummet in the foreign exchange. Likewise, excess rubles rendered the currency virtually worthless within Soviet borders. We heard the news accounts of soaring inflation rates that threatened to crush this struggling nation. The

prime minister was attempting to implement an economic plan that would move the Union toward a "regu-
lated market economy." Since price hikes were an integral part of the plan, the people reacted to the price
hikes with panicked buying. When available, they would
buy six times the flour or eight times the macaroni
needed. The plan called for food to double in price, with
some goods tripling.

Each day was a desperate struggle for survival.
Crime rose 31.8 percent nationwide in 1989, with the
big cities hit hardest. Iron doors and bars for the windows were in constant demand. Fist fights in the markets were commonplace as shoppers brawled over scarce
goods. Many starved while farmers buried their goods,
protesting the low state prices.

Could these people look beyond the daily battle for
existence to see the hope of Christ? Would their vision
be too clouded by the challenges of the day?

Arriving in Riga, Latvia, at 3:00 A.M., we felt like
thieves in the night. It is a city of 1.5 million, yet the
streets were deserted. The city looked abandoned. An
eerie feeling swept over me as we drove by the wreck-
age of a deserted car in the middle of the road. We felt
like time travelers who had just entered the 1940s or
1950s. Visions of old World War II movies flashed
through my mind as I studied the streets. Even at 3:00
A.M., comparable cities in the United States show some
sign of life. New York never sleeps. Riga was a sleeping
giant.

This city, in its heyday, was a key trading center,
thanks to its strategic location along the southern Baltic. Hidden from tourists for more than half a century,
its beautiful European architecture bears the scars of
wars and invasions. Its steepled skyline boasts of
Latvia's rich religious heritage. Today, touring old Riga,
walking the cobbled streets past the Domkirk, you can
still see barricades plastered with graffiti. The messages speak of freedom and this nation's commitment
to protect the precious identity taken from it in 1941.

The Metropole, our home for the next ten days, was the third best hotel in the city, but it could have passed for a ghetto dwelling in downtown Raleigh. We met our host, briefly exchanged greetings, unloaded the equipment, and started to our rooms. The hotel had no air conditioning. Our alternatives were to swelter in the heat or open the window to the August night and thousands of thirsty mosquitoes. Roaches were everywhere, and some team members shared their dwelling with vermin of varied descriptions. No one complained. After all that we saw God do to bring us to this place, the conditions in the hotel were of little importance. We knew we were in the center of His will, and nothing would rob us of His joy. The fire to share His love and truth overshadowed any physical consideration. The desire to be a vessel of His healing balm to these desperate, hurting people made all the rest pale in comparison.

Embarking upon a missions trip, one thinks that the questions of housing, food, and facilities are extremely important. But God quickly makes those things irrelevant to surrendered hearts. His spiritual blessings and faithfulness inspired us to prioritize accordingly. The lack of physical comforts becomes insignificant, vanishing from view as God moves. This was our promised land.

3

"Do not say, I am a youth, because everywhere I send you, you shall go, and all that I command you, you shall speak. Do not be afraid of them, for I am with you to deliver you," declares the Lord.

(Jer. 1:7-8)

A Glimpse of God's Healing

The first morning in Riga, our host informed us that we had a performance in his church that night. My initial reaction was that our ministry was outreach, not performing to the churches. We said from the outset that our calling was to go to the people, to evangelize in the marketplace. Our strategy included their theaters, schools, hospitals, parks, and youth camps.

Our host and the pastor of this church were insistent in their invitation. In an effort not to offend anyone, I agreed. After breakfast, we met for prayer, worship, and preparation in the Scriptures. Every day we sought the discipline learned in Helsinki. We were determined not to miss what God required of us or to make any assumptions. We were not to make the mistake of just doing what seemed right without consulting God. The lessons of Helsinki were bestowed upon us to use, and we faithfully employed them.

Ironically, the church met in a big circus tent. While setting up to perform, the team was approached by some older women, or *babushkas*, who reprimanded them with wagging fingers and vehement language. Through the translator, they admonished us, saying that our ministry was of the devil and clowns did not belong in the church. Many walked out before the service began.

Legalism and the traditions of men were prevalent

in this Pentecostal Russian congregation. There was such a visible struggle between the youth, now in their twenties and thirties, who wanted to reach out to their world, and the older people who were products of tradition.

The team members were visibly shaken and not looking forward to the performance. I stood on the platform waiting to introduce the show while the people were seated. Scanning the audience while I breathed a prayer, I realized that many of the *babushkas* were seated directly in front of the stage. Studying the faces of these older saints, I could almost visualize the history of the persecuted church—what they must have witnessed in their lifetime. During the tenth century, Vladimir, Grand Duke of Kiev, considered every major religion—Islam, Judaism, Roman Catholicism, and Byzantine Orthodoxy. He adopted Byzantine Orthodoxy, as historian Michael Phillips wrote, for its "liturgy, its shapes, its paintings, its vestments, its Byzantine architecture, its tradition, not for the rational truth of its message or its theology. They came to believe that concrete beauty rather than abstract theological ideas contained the essence of the Christian message."

Although hollow in content and a puppet of the czar, the Orthodox Church's religious heritage shaped the landscape of the Republics. Shrines guarded the gateways of villages, often the most imposing structures of the communities and always kept in immaculate condition. Peasants and gentry alike frequented the churches to light candles before the sacred icons for themselves or family members.

As time progressed, true Christian churches did emerge in tacit opposition to the shallow practices of the czar's established religion. Although forced underground by conflicts with the Orthodox Church, the numbers of true believers increased dramatically. However, the October Revolution of 1917 brought an end to religious life in all form and substance. The oppressive Soviet regime branded believers and Orthodox church members alike as counter-revolutionaries. Large scale arrests of clergy were common, and many received harsh prison terms or were put to death for their faith. Many of the priests who were not imprisoned were forced to become traitors to their church and assist the KGB in the perpetration of its reign of terror.

Cathedrals and monasteries were nationalized, plundered, and transformed into warehouses and prisons. Those left intact were nothing more than "museums of liturgical antiquity." The religious education of children was a crime. Parents were imprisoned or committed to psychiatric hospitals for passing down religious convictions to their progeny.

The women who sat before me were of the age to have witnessed much of the terror wreaked on the church. They had persevered. Moreover, their faith had persevered. As I finished my introduction and the musical began, many of the *babushkas* stood and walked out. Why such a reaction? The answers have become clear to me. Active public evangelism of any kind was unheard of. Use of music and the arts certainly was inconceivable under Communist control since simple survival claimed every energy.

The team could not help but be distracted by the angry protest of these religious matriarchs. Yet, they regained their composure like true professionals and concentrated on the performance. Three children and four adults came forward that night to accept Christ. Despite all the distractions, God moved mightily in their hearts, and the determination illumined their faces as they walked the dirt aisle.

Back at the hotel, the team expressed concern about the obvious chasm demonstrated in this congregation. Our translator tried to console us by dismissing it as a typical reaction of the older women. Pastor Peter and the young men in leadership only encouraged us and were excited at the prospect of having us minister again. This time they would distribute flyers in all of the many high-rise apartment complexes that surrounded the church. We prayed, and found comfort in the knowledge that God moved mountains to bring us to this place. And in spite of the problems, He gave us seven new sisters in Christ.

On our first Sunday in Latvia, I was to deliver the morning sermon at the tent church. When informed of my task the night before, I was hesitant. I felt more than a little inadequate to address people who had endured such hardship. What did I know about their suffering? What could a young man from the comforts of America tell these people about their walk with Christ in a nation still hostile to their beliefs?

As the team and I prayed for guidance, God gave me a two-fold message based upon 2 Chronicles 7:14: "If my people who are called by my name, will humble themselves and pray and seek my face and turn from their wicked ways, then will I hear from heaven and will forgive their sin and will heal their land." This nation desperately needed a spiritual resurgence, but it would only occur when the church repented and sought God's face. The older members of the congregation needed to release their young people to reach the generations to come, undergirding their efforts with prayer. The young people needed to accept the challenge of investing their lives in God and eternal endeavors.

A concentrated time of intercession followed discussion of the service. We prayed for God's blessing and asked Him to give us favor with the pillars of the church. The years of persecution had inspired such a survival mentality that it even prompted them to distort Scripture relating to public evangelism and outreach. For instance, they believed that giving out Bibles and tracts to non-Christians was casting your pearl before swine. This distortion of Scripture caused the church to atrophy. Slavic Ministries' Director Al Akimoff once told me that it was like a person bedridden from an extended illness who finds that his legs have withered from inactivity. He requires rehabilitation to learn to walk again. Similarly, the Christian churches in the Soviet Union atrophied from inactivity during the years of oppression and needed instruction and encouragement to begin anew. Seventy years is a long time without practice in the areas of outreach, active evangelism, and discipleship.

Standing on the platform, the sharp contrasts between the old and young loomed over the service. The young people's choir sang contemporary worship songs. Elderly gentlemen would respond by leading old hymns. Could this chasm be healed?

Studying the choir composed of all these young adults, I recognized the validity of my message. The young were trying to sprout their wings of faith, and the old people were still captives of a survival mode. The young people were excited to have us back, and the old were ready for our departure.

Prior to my message, we decided to play the Russian Hosanna tape, *Heal Our Land*. I told them we had a song we would like for them to hear and put the tape in our sound system. The choir recognized it immediately and began to sing. We sang in English, and they in Russian. Tears filled our eyes as we witnessed the unity of the Holy Spirit among believers from two nations who were raised in fear of one another. As the second verse began, "I bow my knee," I knelt and continued to sing, attempting to demonstrate my sincerity in working to see the words of the song come to fruition.

After the song, I stood off to the side, waiting for my introduction. Out of the corner of my eye, I noticed a *babushka*, one who appeared to be a leader in the congregation, get up from her seat and hurry to our translator's side. She began to speak in rapid Russian. I can remember thinking, "Oh no, not another rebuke!" Our translator listened with little expression and no intention of translating. When she finished her message, she pointed to me and insisted that Valare translate. In a dry tone, he said, "This lady says you are anointed. When you knelt during that song, she saw an angel hovering over you and he put his hands on your shoulders. She says, 'You are anointed of God.'" I shared my message with confidence that morning—not confi-

dence in myself or my abilities, but confidence in what
God was doing in this church and in this country. The
healing that began with the words of that *babushka*
was but a glimpse of the healing He planned for the
nation.

My message began with an explanation of the gospel with simple stories and illustrations. As I spoke, a
forty-year-old Soviet man with a strong, stocky build
walked the dirt aisle. The protocol of the service mattered not to this determined man. He felt the conviction of the Holy Spirit, and he responded. With a resolve that only the Spirit can give, he journeyed to the
front and waited patiently as tears flowed down the
lines in his face. I continued to share the gospel while
he stood looking up at me. When the time came for the
invitation, he earnestly prayed for God to change his
life. His tears flowed freely. This man was a vivid
example of the nation's thirst for the gospel.

As planned, the second part of my message was on
the need for revival in the land. Addressing the young
people, I challenged them to offer themselves as God's
vessels, willing to do what He required while counting
the cost. I asked how many would be so committed.
Seventy stood throughout the congregation. We prayed
together.

I then addressed my attention to the older members of the congregation, asking how many would pray
for, encourage, and release these young people into
ministry. Miraculously, all the old people stood. Again,
we prayed. It was as if the breath of God swept across
the whole tent as a new wave of healing and impetus
was set into motion. After our second prayer, the pastor approached the stage and told me that the older
ladies wanted the team to pray for them. We had come
full circle. We were witnessing the consummation of
the healing process. A line formed, the team came
forward, and we prayed for each individual.

Sunday evening we again ministered at the tent
church, but it was an outreach for the whole surround-
ing community. Sveta and her sister, Alena, came to

see the show for the first time. The unifying work of
the Holy Spirit during the Sunday morning service
allowed us to minister unencumbered that evening,
and the message bore great fruit. At the invitation,
sweet Sveta shot her arm in the air without hesitation,
and Alena followed. How beautiful to look back over
God's omnipotent orchestration of the events that led
to their decisions that night. Whatever heartache Sveta
suffered from that point forward, she would never again
suffer alone. Later, I learned that Sveta had come full
circle as well. She had been resistant to the gospel for
years, but that night was the culmination of God's
wooing her into His open arms. His embrace covered
the hurts buried in her past.

During this service, I met a Mongolian man from
Tashkent in the Republic of Tajikistan. He and his
entire family came forward at the invitation. I mentioned the Bible, and he queried, "What is Bible?" Immediately, I felt the sting of conviction as I thought
about the Bibles on my shelves at home and my taking
their availability for granted. These people were starved
for truth in a society that relied on the ability of deceit
to manipulate its people. Consider this poignant example of the search for truth as told by one Soviet
citizen in a secular Russian magazine:

> I just turned over the last page of a great book, and
> I am overcome by feelings of gratitude and happi-
> ness. But there are some bitter questions which
> remain unanswered. Why only now? Why so late?
> Half of my life is gone. Oh, if it could only have
> been ten years earlier! At the age of 30 I was able
> to read the Gospel for the very first time.

> It was entirely by chance that this small book fell
> into my hands, and I approached it with purely
> literary curiosity. I was gripped by what I read and
> it became clear that the value of this book is not to
> be underestimated. Gradually I began to boil with
> indignation. To think that such a treasure had been
> hidden from me? Who decided, and on what grounds,
> that this book was harmful to me?

In our time of unrest and brokenness, when crystal palaces turn out to be cardboard shacks, when once-majestic kings are now covered with shame, when under the granite edifices are unstable foundations of clay, then I know that there is a book to which I can always return, and it will help, comfort and support me in the darkest hour.

There is a God-given longing for the truth in every man that cannot be snuffed out, smothered, or destroyed. We were reminded of this reality each and every time we ministered to this deprived people.

We invited Sveta to worship with us the next morning at our usual early gathering in the hotel. The English lyrics were strange to her ears, but the Spirit of the Lord captured her with the language of the heart. She wept throughout the service, releasing all her hurt to God for His cleansing. I wondered how long it had been since this young woman cried. As I reached out my hand to pray with her, she pressed it to her face. In moments, it was wet with her tears. Another team member knelt with her, gently holding Sveta as she continued to sob. Oh God, how many Svetas are waiting in this land—waiting to hear that they can make it another day, that there is abundant hope for the future?

4

A young man or woman cannot be a Communist youth unless he or she is free of religious convictions.

(Vladimir Ilyich Lenin)

4

The Sons and Daughters of Atheists

That evening we traveled to Jurmala, Latvia, to arrange outreaches in the Pioneer youth camps. Scott asked me before I left what the team should do that evening. His suggestion was to get the remainder of the souvenir shopping out of the way during this free time to ensure focus for the rest of our stay. A sensible proposal, but I encouraged him to seek the Lord.

"Remember what the Lord taught us. We are to take nothing for granted," I said. We learned in the spiritual boot camp of Helsinki that ministry is a two-fold process. First, we must determine God's will. Then we must be willing to allow Him to do whatever He deems necessary in and through our lives to see His will, His vision, become reality. Scott understood and gathered the team together for worship and prayer, making them available for whatever God required.

It was my understanding when we left the hotel that we were arranging a future time of ministry to one of the thirty Pioneer youth camps in Jurmala. After some initial business was discussed, I asked our host, "When would you like to schedule this performance?" His answer shocked me. The outreach was for that night. It was 5:30 P.M., and we were thirty minutes from our hotel. When we returned, the equipment would

have to be picked up at another location; it takes one-
and-a-half hours of preparation before we can perform.

I began praying that if God had this performance
for us, the team would still be in the hotel when we
returned. Otherwise, they would be scattered all over
Riga and outreach would be impossible. As I prayed, I
recognized that it would truly be a miracle if the team
had remained behind and waited. There would be no
doubt that they had heard God's voice.

Back at the hotel, I ran the five flights of stairs to
our rooms. Throwing open the door, I found Scott sitting on his bed reading the Bible. "Where is everyone?"
I asked. Scott explained that as they prayed for God's
direction, he instructed them to study the book of Jude.
The plan was to study the book for thirty minutes and
then meet to finish the shopping. Five more minutes
and they would have been out shopping on what they
thought was their only night off!

The team quickly assembled to leave, anxious for
their first outreach at a Pioneer camp. Responding to
our hearts' cry to be used by Him, God intervened in
circumstances beyond our control and orchestrated the
entire outreach. Never had I felt so covered by His
sovereign hand. We moved quickly, yet the fast pace
did not cloud the realization that nothing short of God's
divine intervention could have caused us to be in this
position. We were on the threshold of ministry unheard
of only months before.

I wept on the way to the camp as I read God's
promise to us in Joshua 1. Immediately after an intense time of prayer, holding fast to God's promises,
our Soviet translator leaned back over the seat and
said, "These children will not understand you. They
are the sons and daughters of atheists and will not
understand what you share about Jesus Christ and the
Bible."

As I think back on this statement, I am reminded of
the dramatic importance of our mission. The generation to which we minister is destined to assume the
roles of teachers, legislators, cabinet members, busi-

nessmen, homemakers, mechanics, clerks, and voters. Every decision tendered from each of the Republics' legislatures will one day be in the hands of these children. The question is not when will they capture power, for the seizure is inevitable. The appropriate question is what will they do with the power placed in their hands.

Proverbs 14:34 reads: "Righteousness exalts a nation, but sin is a disgrace to any people." On which side of this proverb will the Commonwealth of Independent States fall? Will they be recipients of God's blessings as they repent and follow His ways, or will they serve themselves His judgment as a nation with its back turned on Him?

Each nation's future is solely determined by the conviction with which its children are raised. The course of this nation's tomorrows is steered by the navigation set on the hearts and minds of future generations. What will sparkle in their eyes as truth? What will ring true in their hearts? With what resilience and determination will they defend right? What will they let pass as acceptable and tolerable? To what heights will this new society's standards soar; or to what depths will society sink? Will righteousness exalt the Commonwealth?

When studying what shapes the attitudes and beliefs of American children, the family is the place to begin and remains the prevailing influence throughout a person's life. Our nation gives families the autonomy to mold individuals with a personal heritage of ethnic, religious, and cultural allegiances. When studying the children of the Soviet Union, we find a quite different phenomenon. Families inevitably have some influence, but the Soviet Motherland worked diligently to secure the state's role as the principal dictator of its citizenry's values. Its efforts at political socialization were carried out from cradle to grave by institutional agents of behavior and value modification.

The state's level of success in molding a homogeneous population is subject to question. Nevertheless, we can anticipate as we minister that the attitudes and beliefs of the children were significantly influenced by the controlled society in which they were raised.

Public Schools

The public school system was the first agent of socialization encountered by a child. The *Literary Gazette* of the Soviet Union asserted:

> It is in the schools, at the desk, in the first class, that the foundations for a Communist outlook are laid in future Soviet citizens. The country entrusts the school with its most treasured possessions—its children—and no one should be allowed to indulge in the slightest deviation from the principles of the Communist materialistic upbringing of the new generation.

As early as nursery school, classrooms echoed with the praises of the Bolshevik Revolution as little children recited rhymes like: "November seventh, it is clear is the reddest day in all the year. Through the window look ahead, everything outside is red." The first page in a child's alphabet book boasted a picture of Lenin. All language and history books touted the attributes of this infamous tyrant. Children read stories that told of his childhood and praised him for his enlightened values—those values most crucial to the strength of the Union. "Grandfather Lenin" was their role model, and they were to be his helpers. The following poem is just an example of the pristine portrayal of this man: "There is a well-known portrait, upon a classroom wall. We see the face of Lenin so dearly loved by all. His eyes are kind and honest, with cleverness they burn. He tells us, Soviet children, that we must learn and learn."

Strict participation was required during all of the Party holidays. Children marched in parades and sang the prescribed patriotic songs. Memorizing the hymn of the Soviet Union for such occasions was the first activity of the first day of the first grade. Training for life in a society of collectives required that children compete, not as individuals, but as teams. Rows in a classroom competed as did classrooms in a school and schools in a region. Children wore uniforms to drown any image of individualism. They were never to appear unique from other students in appearance or behavior.

During adolescence, Soviet youth were subject to more intense indoctrination. The constitution of the U.S.S.R. stated, "The basic duties of Soviet citizens are to obey the law, to approach social responsibility honestly, and to respect the rules of socialist society." The schools were to ensure that Soviet youth understood their responsibility to the socialist state and to prepare them to assume their roles as productive workers in the economy.

Instructors bowed their knee to the party in their teaching and included the prescribed political messages. Soviet educator N.P. Kuzin explained in 1974:

> Under the present conditions of the school, the task of inculcating a scientific Marxist-Leninist world view, which is founded on a position of Communist Party-mindedness, is a part of the process of instruction in every subject. However, subjects in the social and political cycle—history (domestic and world), economic and political geography, social studies—hold special significance in the formation of the pupils' understanding of the laws of social development and in their inculcation with strong civic feelings and with a sense of social standards in conformity with the norms of socialist society.

In the spirit of "Party-mindedness," facts were manipulated to glorify the Revolution and to tout the Bolsheviks as saviors of the working people. Accurate presentations of historical events were denounced as nothing more than "bourgeois objectivism."

Instruction in the Marxism-Leninism concept of the individual's role in a collective began in the early years of schooling. All emphasis was placed upon the student's willingness to subordinate his interests and pursuits to those of the student collective. In fact, the definition of self-discipline as explained by one Soviet educator is "the ability to, as well as the habit of, controlling one's behavior, of subordinating it to the rules and demands of the collective and of the society, and of performing in accordance with social responsibilities." The practice of this discipline destroyed personal initiative and hindered creativity, reducing the individual to nothing more than a spoke in the wheel, worthless outside of his contribution to the whole.

The student collective was designed to mature the adolescent in this discipline by developing habits that would evolve into the internal motivation to modify behavior. Soviet educators knew that learning by participation was a much more effective tool in behavior modification than simply instructing them on the obligations and responsibilities of adulthood. Punishments were to be administered by the collective or the teacher with the support of the collective. This practice stressed the supremacy of the group over the interests and/or actions of the individual. Some forms of punishment in the collective sense included a notice in the school paper, an announcement over the school intercom, a letter to the parents written by the collective, and a public reprimand. Measures such as these encouraged children to tow the party line and follow the rules blindly or risk the wrath of friends who frowned upon, and could possibly face punishment themselves for, their "rebellion."

Children quickly learned that conformity and blind loyalty were the rewarded forms of behavior. Evaluation of the happenings around them was strictly forbidden. Individuals were considered nothing more than "carriers of ideas"—carriers who needed to learn not how to think but what to think if they were to be productive automatons of the socialist state. In order to prepare students to enter the work force, a curricular approach to introducing them to life in a collective, be it agricultural, industrial, or pedagogical, was encouraged in every school Khrushchev once said:

> One of the most important tasks of Communist education is to reinforce in everyone's mind the fact

that since all accomplishments of the Soviet man benefit him and society, no man can live without working productively. When, out of concern for his comrades, he approaches his assignments with honesty and works diligently at them while keeping up with the set time schedule, he manifests collaboration as well as reciprocal aid, both of which are relevant among people in our new society.

To accomplish the prescribed objective, for example, students were systematically exposed to life in a factory collective. They learned that this attitude and life of blind service was the spirit of communism and "that work for the sake of society is the holiest duty of every individual."

Integral in the education of Soviet youth in Marxism-Leninism is instruction in atheism. According to Lenin, "Marxism cannot be conceived without atheism. We would add here that atheism without Marxism is incomplete and inconsistent." In the minds of Soviet leaders, atheism and Marxism go hand in hand. They are inseparable. It is impossible to demonstrate total loyalty to the state if you harbor any allegiances to God. Lenin also said, "A young man or woman cannot be a Communist youth unless he or she is free of religious convictions." The *Young Bolshevik* publication echoed his sentiments when it printed: "If a Communist youth believes in God and goes to Church, he fails to fulfill his duties. This means that he has not yet rid himself of religious superstitions and has not become a fully conscious person (i.e., a Communist)."

In keeping with these beliefs, churches as well as parents were strictly forbidden to provide religious instruction to those under eighteen. In fact, the harshest penalty a person could receive was for instructing children in spiritual matters. Conversely, instruction in atheism was compulsory from kindergarten through the university. The Soviet government invested millions to disseminate an abundance of atheistic publications, films, lectures, and exhibitions to indoctrinate the youth under its reign. As late as October 1984,

Pravda counseled: "It is imperative to carry out more active propaganda of scientific materialistic opinions, pay more attention to atheistic education. . . . The Party is particularly concerned that young people should form firm atheistic convictions."

Children from families with open religious convictions were ridiculed by their classmates. Often they were taunted, harassed, and beaten until parents were forced to remove them from school to ensure their safety. Graduation from secondary school was contingent upon a passing grade in final exams on all subjects including one on society. This exam included the ideals of communism, socialism, the October Revolution, and the foundations of Marxism-Leninism. A student could perform brilliantly on all exams, but if he failed the exam on society, he was barred from the university.

In college, students delved deeply into atheism, the history of the Communist party, the ideology and philosophy of Marxism-Leninism, and the political economy of Marx, Engels, Lenin, and contemporary leaders. At the end of four years, state college exams were given in a student's major field or fields of study and also in the ideological subjects. If a student did not give the appropriate answers on the ideological exams, his diploma was withheld.

An adult pursuing his doctorate went through the same regimen of tests. These exams often included sections on religious beliefs, termed "bourgeois remnants." Students were to critique each of these beliefs and give the Marxist-Leninist basis for the critique. If a student did not pass, he would not be allowed to defend his dissertation. Every scientist, medical doctor, and professional who has a Ph.D. had to pass in-depth exams in Marxism-Leninism, communism, socialism, and atheism.

Party Structure

The Communist party structure worked in concert with the public school system to introduce collectivism and begin to mold children into productive socialists. At the age of seven, soon after children entered the first grade, they were inducted into the first party tier, the Young Octobrists. Membership was virtually universal for children seven to nine. In this organization, children began to learn that the supreme virtue is service to the state and the development of a revolutionary mentality. A portion of the Octobrists anthem reads:

> We are the happy kids;
>
> We are the Octobrists.
>
> Our name we can explain.
>
> It's our contribution to the Revolution.
>
> We respect our elders;
>
> We protect our youngers.
>
> We are all precise;
>
> We love morning exercise.

With the child's introduction to the student collective operating in every classroom and the peer collective of this party structure, the family was swiftly replaced as the primary agent of socialization. Soviet society is structured to replace the family with institutional surrogates that mold the child into the new Soviet person, shaping his soul, heart, and intellect. Parents were considered nothing more than custodians of their progeny. Future generations were owned by the state. Parents were frequently reminded of their supportive role when the peer collective would require a report concerning a child's behavior at home.

Classroom emphasis on conformity was nurtured by the party structure. Successful Octobrist leadership inspired in the child a desire to please the party above all else. Here a child began to mature into the ideal Soviet citizen, totally politicized in all his actions and thoughts and reconciled to the party's guidance on the most personal aspects of life. Hopes and dreams were no longer his own but the property of the state. An exemplary Young Octobrist envisioned himself as a productive member of the whole, ready to serve wherever he was needed.

At the age of nine, a Young Octobrist became a Young Pioneer and remained in this second tier until he was fifteen. Again, membership was universal, although the better students were inducted first with special recognition, followed by the rank and file nine-year-olds some weeks later.

Life in a peer collective was intensified during the years as a young Pioneer. The belief was that the "earlier the child is exposed to a life in a collective, the greater are his chances of growing up to be a real Communist." Therefore all endeavors concentrated on translating the concepts of Marxism-Leninism into language and activity that children could understand. The games introduced were to emphasize collectivism. The purpose of every activity was designed to develop collectivist instincts in a child, whose natural inclination is toward individualism. Every thought, word, and deed was to be permeated with the Pioneer spirit, which is love for the Soviet Motherland and the determination "to live, to study, and to struggle, as Lenin willed and as the Communist Party teaches." If a Pioneer noticed that an independent student group was forming around a common interest such as nature or the environment, it was that Pioneer's duty to infiltrate the group with the spirit of communism.

Inculcating a sense of duty to the Communist party and the Soviet Motherland was of primary importance. Each Pioneer group was to embark upon some "socially necessary" task. They could clean classrooms, tutor fellow students, or collect war relics for a museum glorifying the Revolution.

The final tier before membership in the Communist party was membership in the Komsomol or Communist Youth League. While membership in the Octobrists and Pioneers was virtually universal, a degree of selectivity was exercised in Komsomol membership. At the age of fifteen, a youth had to be invited for membership by a Komsomol member of at least two years or a member of the Communist party and also give evidence of positive character traits. He would remain in this organization until the age of twenty-seven when he would or would not be asked to join the party.

Komsomol members were urged to take leadership positions with the younger party tiers. The spoken rationale was that it would be easier for the Octobrists and Pioneers to relate to the Komsomol members. However, the primary reason delved much deeper into the Soviet psyche. Giving the young Komsomol member responsibility for the indoctrination of others in the ideals of the state contributed in large measure to his own indoctrination. Placing him in a leadership role where it was necessary for him to convey party ideals with conviction forced him to take ownership of them. He would not be able to live with himself otherwise. Psychologists agree that this mandatory role-playing socializes a person more quickly than if he remains on the receiving end of someone else's indoctrination efforts.

Other "socially necessary" duties included giving party-line lectures at a factory or participating in political or literary debates, tutoring younger children in their studies, offering to clean lab equipment at the university, performing needed factory or farm work during the summer or on holidays, and continuing their study of Marxism-Leninism and the writings of contemporary Soviet leaders.

In addition, they were to continue monitoring their peers as they learned in the Pioneers. If they detected a certain anti-party sentiment on a college campus, in a factory or farm collective, or even on the street corner among friends, they were to defend the party and convince the rebels of their error. The former Soviet official Victor Kravchenko described the understood responsibility of the Komsomol member in his expose, *I Chose Freedom*. "As a Komsomol, I must never lose a chance to preach the happy life to come, to explain away immediate troubles." Being a faithful party member was a full-time obligation that could benefit a Communist youth if done well or contribute to his downfall if performed poorly in the reproving eyes of his party boss.

The price was high for those who refused membership in the party structure. Children who did not participate were harassed by their peers and faced the possibility of being taken from their parents. Students graduating from secondary school could forget about entering a university if they were not a Komsomol member. The dissident author Vladimir Bukovsky wrote:

> When I was fourteen, which is when they start taking everyone into the Komsomol, I refused to join. "What's the matter? Do you believe in God?" they asked me curiously, but I refused to give any explanation. They pressed me for a very long time, because I was a good student and it was the accepted thing for all the good ones to be in the Komsomol, but they didn't get anywhere and in the end gave up. "Watch out," said my friends, "you'll find it harder to get into the university."

If parents wanted a "decent" life for their progeny, they performed as faithful members of the party and enrolled their children at the first opportunity. Anything less than total allegiance, or the appearance thereof, brought grave consequences upon the offenders.

Religious Persecution

The final birthright bestowed upon all children of the Soviet Union that imprisons their hearts, and more important, the hearts of the parents who raise them, is a grave history of religious persecution. The systematic legacy of indoctrination perpetrated by the schools and cradle-to-grave party structure was more than adequate to mold a child into a staunch Soviet and atheist. Coupling this intricate propaganda system with the grave acts perpetrated against the church, clergy, and believers virtually ensured that neither parents nor their children would venture forth in search of spiritual truth.

Karl Marx's spoken objective in his conception of dialectical materialism was to "dethrone God." His ultimate desire was to develop a theory of nature that completely repudiated all forms of religion. Marx's cohort Frederick Engels gloated that with the discovery of the Communist laws of nature, "the last vestige of a Creator external to the world is obliterated."

As Marx and Engels began to conceive the idea of a revolutionary society struggling against the ruling classes, the war on religion became integral to their cause. Marx described religion as "the sigh of the oppressed creature, the heart of a heartless world, just as it is the spirit of spiritless conditions. It is the opium of the people."

The Marxist zealot Vladimir Ilyich Lenin declared war on religion in Russia even before the Bolshevik Revolution: "Religion and communism are incompatible in theory as well as in practice. . . . We must fight religion." After the Revolution, he swiftly acted to constrain the influence of the church. Between December 1917 and the end of January 1918, all the land of the Russian Orthodox church was nationalized along with the ornaments and icons given by faithful members. Bank accounts that belonged to religious organizations were nationalized, and all religious instruction was removed from the schools, including instruction on Russia's rich religious heritage.

Echoing Marx's belief that religion is an opiate of the people, Lenin asserted, "Religion is a kind of spiritual gin in which the slaves of capital drown their human shape and their claims to any decent human life." The practice of religion threatened the course of the revolution. As discussed earlier, the Communist party expected nothing less than total allegiance to its imperialistic plan for the world. The Russian Commissioner of Education under Lenin stated, "We hate Christians and Christianity. Even the best of them must be considered our worst enemies. Christian love is an

obstacle to the development of the revolution. Down
with love of one's neighbor! What we want is hate. . . .
Only then can we conquer the universe."

Records indicate that between 1918 and 1920 thousands of priests were murdered or imprisoned, 12,000
laymen were reported killed for religious activities,
and 673 monasteries of the 1,025 in existence in 1914
were dissolved. Since monastic service was considered
the highest calling in the Russian Orthodox Church,
attacking the monasteries cut the Orthodox Church off
at the knees. Angered that the Orthodox hierarchy
opposed the state's confiscation of church valuables,
Lenin signed an official order of 22 February 1922,
which stated:

> At the next Party Congress a secret session should
> be organized jointly with the leading members of
> the GPU (predecessor of the KGB), the Commis-
> sariat of Justice and the Revolutionary Tribunal. A
> secret decision of the Congress should approve a
> mercilessly resolute confiscation of church valu-
> ables. The more members of the reactionary bour-
> geoisie we manage to shoot the better. It is pre-
> cisely now that we must give such a lesson to these
> characters that they would not dare to think of any
> resistance for at least the next few decades.

Komsomol members were tasked with stripping
churches in the villages of their icons and liturgical
valuables and making them into grain storehouses.
The imprisonment and "physical liquidation" of clergy
and church workers became an everyday occurrence.
During Lenin's reign of terror, it is estimated that
2,691 married priests, 1,962 monks, 3,447 nuns, and
an unknown number of laymen and women were killed.
Dissidents disappeared off the city streets, from their
beds in the middle of the night, off the assembly line at
the factory, from the markets, and even off the operating table in the middle of surgery. The people lived in
horror, never knowing when or how officials might
seize them. They could be arrested by a religious pil-
grim they housed for the night, the meterman who

checked their electric meter, a taxi driver, a bicyclist, a railway conductor, or the manager of a movie theater.

At Lenin's hand, the legislative machine curtailed the influence of religious institutions. He issued an ordinance that all schools, academies, and institutions owned by religious organizations were to be turned over to the People's Commissariat of Education. All state funds to religious establishments were to cease. A decree, entitled "On Separation of Church from State and School from Church," put all authority over religious instruction and building in the hands of the state. The registration of births, marriages, and deaths, previously handled by the church, was secularized. All religious services and icons were banned from public buildings. All religious groups were required to be registered. Discretion over whether registration would be permitted or refused was left to the Soviet government. A Council for Religious Affairs was established and charged with monitoring the activities of all groups. Representatives attended all meetings and carried out routine inspections. Groups and churches were never without surveillance.

Lenin's successors shared his hatred for religion and religious dissidents. Joseph Stalin once penned:

> Have we suppressed the reactionary clergy? Yes, we have. The unfortunate thing is that it has not been completely liquidated. Anti-religious propaganda is a means by which the complete liquidation of the reactionary clergy must be brought about. Cases occur when certain members of the Party hamper the complete development of anti-religious propaganda. If such members are expelled it is a good thing because there is no room for such "Communists" in the ranks of the Party.

Stalin took Lenin's reign of terror one step further in the 1930s and attempted the physical destruction of the church as an institution. Churches and cathedrals were used for secular government purposes, and Sunday was eliminated as a day of worship. Factories ran day and night, seven days a week, with workers rotat-

ing their days off. The Union of Militant Atheists
boasted an active membership of two-and-one-half million.

On 22 August 1941, the publication *Soviet War
News* published the following statistics: In 1917, there
had been 47,457 Orthodox churches, 50,960 Orthodox
priests, and 130 bishops. By 1941 there were only 4,225
churches, 5,665 priests, and 28 bishops. The infamous
purge trials of Stalin saw tens of thousands killed that
were thought to oppose his rule. Clergy and sectarian
believers were sentenced to labor camps, and some
were sent to desolate islands with no food.

Solzhenitsyn wrote of the wholesale slaughter of
Christians: "There was a multitude of Christians: prisoner transports and graveyards, prisoner transports
and graveyards. Who will count those millions?" According to Solzhenitsyn, religious believers, many of
them nuns, were favored for work in the penalty compounds of the gulag. The labor in these compounds was
designed to kill. In many cases, they were required to
work in the swamps with their feet always in water.
The guards were ordered to shoot to kill. Clouds of
mosquitoes would consume the workers, and they would
emerge from the swamps covered with welts and scabs,
their eyelids swollen. Lime and rock quarry work was
saved for the penalty workers. "All the heaviest of the
heavy jobs, all the most unbearable of the unbearable
jobs—that was penalty labor."

Khruschev came to power with the same vehement
resolve to eliminate religious observance. He even
boasted in the late 1950s that by 1965 religion in the
Soviet Union would be obsolete. He added that upon
the realization of his goal he would insist that at least
one Christian be preserved and placed in a museum for
all to see the last of an extinct species.

Despite the incessant efforts of Lenin and his followers, religion did not die in the Soviet Union. Believers were strengthened in their faith even in the gulag,
and those still free took their spiritual pilgrimage underground. However, many people bought the lies of

the Soviets and put their hope in communism. With this blind act of trust, they also relinquished the spirits of their children. Even in small villages where not one Soviet resided, atheism seemed to stretch its tentacles from Moscow and hold the people captive. The Russian author Maurice Hindus described this phenomenon in his book, *Humanity Uprooted*: "The Revolution seemed to have surcharged the very air with a substance that, when inhaled, automatically burned up religious faith, especially in youth."

Many of those who recognized the deceit of the Soviets still denied their rich spiritual heritage and assumed the life chosen for them by the state. In an effort to protect their children, they joined the Communist party and did not speak of God in their households. They lived as if God was of no pertinence to their daily lives. Survival was the only objective. Some Russian Orthodox Churches succumbed to the state, and some priests served as KGB agents. They turned their backs on the faith and began to hand over the names of people who contacted them desiring to be married in the church or to have their babies christened. These people were subsequently expelled from the party. They lost their jobs and were destined to live under the seemingly omnipotent eye of the KGB.

Not one family was left unscathed by the religious persecution of more than seventy years under Communist rule. Although communism was not delivering all it guaranteed and parents scorned its hollow promises behind closed doors, the hearts of children were still shackled in the ghosts of the past. Valare was right in one respect. The large majority of children in the Soviet Union were still under the atheistic authority of the schools and party structure. Moreover, they were being raised by parents who were atheists by personal conviction or discouraged from searching out spiritual truth by the years of intense persecution suffered by the church. Old habits are hard to break, particularly habitual fear.

5

I will give you the treasures of darkness, and hidden wealth in secret places, in order that you may know that it is I, the Lord, the God of Israel, who calls you by name.

(Isa. 45:2-3)

Treasures of Darkness

Valare may have been correct about the children to whom we would minister, but he knew nothing of the powerful God we serve. As I held tight to His promises, I quietly told our translator that we knew what we were doing. At 8:30 P.M., the staff of the camp began to move the children, ages five to fifteen, into the auditorium while the team completed the finishing touches on their makeup. I tried to interact with some of our curious audience, but I got no response. My smiles were met with nothing but apprehension.

Introducing the show, I told them that Jesus Christ was the reason for our being there. I described the love, joy, and peace that Jesus brings to our hearts and assured them that He offered the same for their lives. Recognizing that many probably had never read the Bible, I explained that our play was based on the story of the prodigal son told by Jesus. As their curious eyes followed my every move, I closed by telling them that if they listened very closely, they would learn things that would change their lives forever. Little did I know how profound that statement would prove to be as the night began to unfold.

The music began, and smiles broke out on all those little faces; laughter echoed through the auditorium, and hands clapped to the songs. Children who were frightened to enter the auditorium were now right at home as they listened to the message of the gospel

through our musical, *The Greatest Star of All*. Midway
through the show, at what we call the Bible song, the
gravity of the event struck me. I turned to Sarah Bandy,
who was running the sound and lights, and expressed,
"I cannot believe what we are doing!" There we were in
a camp formerly used to indoctrinate children in Marxism-Leninism, sharing the gospel.

Zack, the wild animal trainer, picked up the Bible
and said, "I have here the most important book in the
entire world." The Ringmaster chimed in,

> Ladies and gentlemen, children of all ages, we are
> pleased to introduce to you the book beyond all
> books, the blueprint for how to live, the wisdom no
> one else can give. In it, we hear God talk. Through
> it He can teach us how to walk. I speak of none
> other than . . . the Bible!

And then the lyrics of the chorus, "It's the blueprint
for living, it's the book of books about the King of
Kings, a love letter to His children, it is the word of
God." We were sharing Christ in a country that only
one year previous doled out the harshest prison penalty to those who shared Him with children.

At the close of the musical, just before the final
song, Zack turned to the audience and said, "Don't be
left out. You can meet Him too," referring to the "Greatest Star of All," Jesus Christ.

A hush fell over the auditorium as they waited for
the translation. At that moment, something happened
that I will never forget as long as I live. Four hundred
and eighty children and adults responded in unison,
"*Da!*" or "Yes!" Tears streamed down the faces of the
team as they struggled with the words to the finale,
"He's the light of the world, shining down from heaven,
brighter than the morning sun. Messiah, Jesus is His
Name. He's the greatest star of all."

The response was overwhelming. No one looked
around or awaited the approval of his neighbor. Each
one cried out to God with no reservations. The emotion
of the moment gripped each one of us. We had endured
so much to see this fruit! To see such confirmation of

our mission overwhelmed us. We reveled in the culmination of a year's labor. The struggles of recent days seemed so remote and God so omnipotent as every person in the audience, child and staff member alike, prayed the sinner's prayer, committing his life to Jesus Christ.

They may have arrived the sons and daughters of atheists, but they left that modest auditorium new babes in Christ. They were God's creation, and no amount of deceit could obscure His voice. He had formed them in their mothers' wombs, and that day, He broke through the shackles of their hearts—the shackles of Marxism-Leninism, atheism, and fear—and drew them unto Himself as only He could. God's truth could not be concealed; it reigned supreme.

This was the first of many times overseas that God confirmed how incredibly powerful this medium of theater is in sharing the gospel. The music, comedy, drama, costumes, sets, lights, dance, color, and visuals all combine to graphically communicate the gospel. Those in the audience do not just hear songs or hear someone tell about Jesus. They watch as Tiger leaves her friends and goes her own way, following after Harley the Hobo. When she ends up in the cage, they see her sorrow and her repentance. Finally, they witness Zack's selfless devotion to his friend in giving up his most prized possession, his gold pointer, in return for her freedom. Those visuals combine to bring the gospel to life for the children.

When we returned the next day to pick up our equipment, the changes in the children were nothing short of miraculous. Love poured from their hearts in response to the love and affection demonstrated by the team. These children were not yet aware of the changes taking place, but God was transforming their identities. The team treated them as unique creatures in Christ, and they responded to the truths that inspired such treatment. No longer were they in bondage to the teaching that individuals were worthless outside of their contribution to the whole. God's unconditional love completely freed them from the deceit of the past.

Crowding around the team for final good-byes, they savored every moment with their messengers of His love. We presented the director with two Bibles, one for adults and one for children. She presented us with 480 follow-up cards with the names and addresses of children and adults. The children lavished us with precious gifts.

We left our new brothers and sisters in Christ with mixed emotions. It was hard to part, but we rejoiced in the knowledge that this was not good-bye. Their decisions for Christ had insured our meeting again one day. We traveled to another youth camp. The events of the day before inspired in each of us great expectations for this performance. Our first experiences in a government owned and controlled youth camp could not have been greater confirmation that we were exactly where God wanted us. What joy to know that you are in the center of God's will! We were truly "blessed to be a blessing."

This auditorium was a little more modern with stationary folding seats. The audience was a mixture of children from the camp and some from a nearby sanatorium serving youngsters who were victims of the Chernobyl nuclear disaster. These children appeared healthy, but many suffered from debilitating illnesses that have no cure in the Soviet Union. This "superpower" is generations behind the United States in medical technology. In fact, in every respect except militarily, this nation appears to be trapped in the World War II era. Since the Soviet Union was unable to cure most diseases, sanatoriums were established throughout the nation. Many are located in Jurmala along the Baltic Sea because the sea air is thought to have certain healing properties. Children from all over the Soviet Union travel to these sanatoriums in the hope of alleviating the misery of their conditions.

With very few distractions, they spend each day dwelling on the illness that separates them from family and friends. In the natural sense, our musical served as a welcomed reprieve from the monotony and suffering of the day. In the spiritual sense, God in His infinite mercy saw the plight of these children and brought us to minister to them. We knew that some of these youngsters, because of the terminal cancer rifling through their bodies, might never get another chance to hear about the sacrifice of His Son.

During the musical, they sat on the edge of their seats, all eyes fixed on the stage. When Zack gave the invitation, all 250 seats flapped up simultaneously, resounding through the auditorium. It was the echo of "*Da*" from the previous day. How sad, yet at the same time glorious, to witness the spiritual hunger of the children! Sad to think of the years of spiritual deprivation, yet wonderful to see God penetrate their legacy of deceit and draw them unto Him. He was indeed communicating heart to heart.

Sonia met five-year-old Anya after the show. Having seen her stand to accept Christ, Sonia approached her, knelt down, and said, "*Jesus tibia liubit*," Jesus loves you. It was the only phrase Sonia knew, but nothing could have been more appropriate. As she reached out to hug this little one, Anya fell limp, obviously confused by Sonia's advance. These children were not accustomed to demonstrative affection, a truth that was apparent to each of us as we reached out in love.

The following day we returned for our equipment, arriving early to spend a little time with them. While we were singing some American songs in a small, impromptu gathering, in walked little Anya. She marched right over to Sonia and held her hand. Sonia's eyes filled with tears as she knelt down beside her. Before Sonia could embrace her, Anya gave her the biggest hug the little girl could muster and said, "*Jesus tibia liubit, Sonia*."

Missionaries give of themselves; the sacrifices are undeniable. There is very little that is any harder than wholeheartedly obeying God's will no matter what the cost. The only thing more difficult is not obeying. The cost of following Jesus is your life, but as Jim Elliot once wrote, "He is no fool who gives what he cannot

keep to gain what he can never lose." But the sacrifices
cannot compare to the blessings God's servants receive
as they minister to the lost. This moment with Anya
was one that Sonia will never forget, as the love she
demonstrated to this little girl was returned to her
one-hundred-fold. We serve an awesome God.

Each night we met and discussed the events of the
day, giving thanks to God for the victories realized in
the hearts of these people. We also spent time reflecting on the lessons of Helsinki, reviewing our intercession notes and renewing our commitment to be His
vessels.

Our next performance offered an unusual challenge
in that some wanted it to be a media event. We were to
minister at a sanatorium, and they wanted to use our
presence as a publicity stunt. They had arranged for
two television crews—one Latvian and the other American—to film our ministry to these children. We were
told that it would be great press for our ministry. Our
hearts' cry during worship that morning was that they
would not come. We are not adverse to publicity, but
we feared that the children might get lost in the glare
of the lights and the shuffle of people and cameras.

Again, God echoed the promises of Joshua and
Jeremiah in our hearts, and particularly Isaiah 45:2-3:
"I will go before you and will level the mountains, I will
shatter the gates of bronze, and cut through the iron
bars. And I will give you the treasures of darkness, and
hidden wealth in secret places . . ." Our ministry in
that foreign land taught us that the "treasures of darkness" and the "wealth of secret places" were these children. For too long, the Soviet regime held its youth
captive. God was setting the captives free, drawing
them into His everlasting light. They accepted Him
with a joy and excitement that inspired conviction in
our hearts. It was the most natural display of faith. We
were again reminded of Matthew 18:3, "I tell you the
truth, unless you change and become like little children, you will never enter the kingdom of heaven." God
allowed us to boldly walk into the lives of these chil-

dren and share the life and love of His Son, Jesus
Christ. We experienced like never before His heart and
call.

Upon our arrival at the sanatorium, we were encouraged to see no television crews, Latvian or American. Our prayers were faithfully answered. The atmosphere was peaceful, and our time with the children
rich. Evidently, the American crew's equipment was
lost in transit to Riga the day before and the Latvian
crew received poor directions.

With no media to distract attention from the message of the musical and our time with the children, the
day's ministry proved phenomenal. I introduced the
musical as always, proclaiming Jesus as Savior and
Lord. The play began with simultaneous translation,
and the wonderful news of the Gospel was presented to
the children, obviously thirsting for the unconditional
love of Christ. Three hundred stood to ask Him into
their hearts.

Scanning the children as they stood to pray, I caught
a glimpse of a woman in her sixties standing outside
with her hand raised. I had noticed her earlier peering
around one of the speakers. When the children began
to pray, she too bowed her head and repeated the
simple prayer that flowed through the open window to
her waiting ears. Undoubtedly, this older woman understood the decision she made that August afternoon,
but her maturity stood in stark contrast to that of the
other babes in Christ scattered all over the auditorium.
Did they truly understand the significance of the prayer
they repeated? We were seeing such response that it
was tempting to wonder whether they were just standing because that is what they felt was expected of
them.

In an interview after the musical for *Kids* magazine, the writer Laura Watts asked one ten-year-old,
"Sasha, what did you learn from the musical?"

Without hesitation, he responded, "I learned that
Jesus Christ sacrificed His life to redeem us from our
sins."

Laura probed a little further, "Did you ask Jesus into your heart?"

"*Da!*"

"And how did that make you feel?"

"I feel the presence of God inside my heart!" he replied.

Little Sergei eagerly responded to Laura's questions. "I learned from the musical that Jesus Christ has come to earth to teach people and He has sacrificed His life to make people good."

"How did asking Jesus into your heart make you feel?"

"I felt the presence of the Lord inside me."

Fifteen-year-old Alisha had some questions of her own. She desired to be baptized and wanted our assurance that it was the right thing to do. What a blessing to see children so swiftly embrace a commitment made only moments earlier!

Our Bible study the following morning centered on 1 Chronicles 13, 14, and 15, where David first made a mistake in attempting a task simply because it seemed right to him and the people. He did not inquire of God. David transported the ark of God on a new ox cart rather than the manner prescribed by God. When it began to tip, Uzzah reached out to steady it and God struck him dead. Uzzah did what seemed the right thing, but God had commanded that the ark was not to be touched.

In chapter 14, David faced two enemies. Having seen God's response to disobedience, he inquired of the Lord before he went into those battles to receive His permission and His battle plan. Because David was obedient and inquired of God, He delivered both armies into his hands.

Finally, chapter 15 details the account of David's moving the ark according to God's plan. He had learned his lesson, and God was in their midst helping them. We too must diligently inquire of God if we want His blessing and help in our endeavors. We must lay ourselves before Him in preparation for ministry.

As usual, we arrived early to pick up our equipment and spend some time with the children before our next performance. Waiting in the dining hall lobby for a breakfast made with loving hands, we sang worship songs and taught them the words to "Jesus Loves Me." They returned with some songs in their native tongue. After breakfast, we loaded the bus and exchanged some long good-byes and countless addresses. Children appeared with gifts of flowers, pins, trinkets, and cards, demonstrating their affection and heartfelt desire to form enduring bonds of friendship. One little girl searched her belongings and came up empty-handed, so she walked away, removed her earrings, and returned to give them to Sonia. A true demonstration of sacrificial love.

Aleena, a little ten-year-old girl, had been crying for some time, anticipating our departure. As the bus moved off, all the children began crying, waving, and calling to us. We backed down the road to the camp while some kept running and jumping up to the windows to catch one last glimpse of their new American friends. As the children faded from view, little Aleena alternated between waving and burying her red face in her hands, attempting to hide her tears. Several of the boys ran more than one quarter of a mile down the road following us. The atmosphere on the bus was markedly different than any previous time as we gazed out the windows at those precious treasures. Our prayer for God to break our hearts for these children was being answered. The tears flowed. Jesus touched us deeply that day. Perhaps we were gaining a new understanding of Jesus' words that when we receive the least of these, we receive Him. We saw Him in their faces. We saw Him reflected in their smiles and in their tears. We felt His hand as their little hands grasped ours, His arms as these little children embraced us, His sacrificial love as they gave us precious gifts.

I knew Jesus was smiling. I knew those were His tears falling from my eyes.

Only the quiet sobs broke the uncharacteristic silence. I looked up at the team. Their eyes were glazed and faces red. In their expressions, I saw God answering this prayer in a new way, with new depth. What irony! How could our hearts be so full, yet breaking?

We left that place, but our love remained. We truly saw Jesus that day in the faces of new brothers and sisters not yet twenty-four-hours old. An ocean separated our homelands, language was an obstacle, but Jesus' love traversed every barrier and locked our hearts, united for all eternity. It was just as if He held court there, the children huddling around Him, sitting in His lap, resting their little faces on His shoulders. Every time we think of this special scene, we will choke back the tears. The words will come hard as we tell others the stories and seek to transport them to that place.

I told the team not to despise the emotions but to embrace them. For at that moment when the tears come, the lump will not subside, and we pause to wipe away the tears, our listeners will travel there with us. They will be on the bus, looking through the glass at those precious faces. Through our words and through our tears, others will see the children of the Soviet Union, captives set free by the grace of our Lord. They will see Alisha or Edick jumping for one last glimpse. They will see Aleena trying to hide the tears. They will be reminded that many children still yearn for the love only our Savior can give. Every time we tell the story, it should stir us anew and inspire others to join in answering the desperate need.

Over one hundred people gathered for the first of two performances in a small amphitheater. Many were older children. This musical is obviously designed for a young audience, fourteen and under, but the message is one for all ages. The design does not obscure the truths of the gospel. Time and again, we witnessed the play's strength in ministering to all ages. This was our first time using a second translator for the women's parts. Helena was seventeen and did the parts beautifully. Her emotion captivated the audiences.

A little girl in the back of the crowd mounted her father's shoulders in hopes of getting a better view. Her expression was so tender and unspoiled, but her father's was stern, his thick moustache stationary throughout the performance. Almost the entire audience came forward at the invitation, including the little four-year-old who watched from her father's brawny shoulders. Who says that little preschoolers cannot make meaningful decisions for Christ? That is exactly what Satan wants us to think. Our misconception only gives him more time to work in their lives.

After the prayer, we met little Katya. She came forward and gave the team hugs and flowers. Her father mustered only a faint smile. Little did we know that we would meet that little girl again and witness what the faith of children can do in the lives of parents.

Our next Pioneer camp was said to be the nicest in the area. Indeed it was the nicest facility we visited in Latvia. The director met us and invited us to have supper with them. During the meal, she shared that after hearing about the message and content of our musical, she talked with the children and they seemed excited to have us. She had probed further, asking if they would like to study these things in-depth, and they had responded positively. Thus, she was prepared to invite us for the whole month of August 1991 to conduct Bible studies with the children. Amazing! This director, who in the past organized and perhaps taught lessons on the virtues of Marxism, extended an invitation for an entire month of teaching the children about Jesus and nurturing their relationships with Him.

In the midst of final prep for the show, one of the team members called me over to the corner of the stage. Propped against the wall was a large canvas portrait of Lenin, a hole thrust in the bottom. Surely this picture once enjoyed a place of prominence in that hall. My mind raced forward to the time when the team would herald the name of Jesus then back to the director's inviting us the following year for more in-depth instruction. God was indeed stirring the hearts of this nation.

Reflecting on this camp and our opportunities to minister there, I am reminded of the man for whom it is named—Yuri Gagarian, the first Russian cosmonaut. He made this infamous statement upon his return from space. "I have been to the heavens, and there is no God." No doubt the children have heard these words many times during their lessons.

At the invitation, many children, teen-agers, and adults came forward to pray. This was the first time that we had room to bring them down front. I know God gloried in those children giving their lives to Christ in a camp dedicated to the memory of a man who renounced Him. "Many are the plans in a man's heart, but the Lord's purpose always prevails" (Prov. 19:21).

After the performance, the director hosted an incredible reception in our honor. Again, she reiterated her invitation and informed me that she had just called Riga to obtain their approval. The decision was ours. God was faithfully giving us the "treasures of darkness" and the "hidden wealth of secret places." Soviet children guarded from the truth, robbed of God's intended blessings, were now hearing of His abundant love and beginning a new life in Him.

I pray America will learn from the mistakes of these people before it is too late. We must not allow the forces of evil to take our treasures and carry them away into darkness. We must faithfully and actively protect our future generations for they are "a heritage from the Lord." Our complacency is Satan's greatest advantage.

After each invitation, I congratulated them on the best decision they would ever make. I explained that God wanted them to grow in their new relationship with Him by continuing to pray and talk to Him and reading and obeying His Word, the Bible.

Our final day of ministry began with worship and Bible study. We reviewed the Scriptures God gave us as signposts along the way—Joshua, Jeremiah, and Isaiah. Knowing that this would be the last time I taught the team before traveling home, I talked with them about all God had entrusted to us in these past days—incredible lessons of His sovereignty, heart, and call in His battle for the hearts of this nation and the world. God called us to treasure these moments in our hearts and to cultivate them as the foundation of our future. I read from Luke 12:31-48, which begins: "Seek for His kingdom, and these things shall be added to you" and ends with, "from everyone who has been given much shall much be required; and to whom they entrusted much, of him they will ask all the more."

God entrusted us with much learning. We saw His hand move faithfully in our midst and faithfully on our behalf. He used these days to make eternal deposits in our hearts, playing out things before us that we would never forget. Now, He was calling us to be stewards of all He gave. These rocks of remembrance were to be the foundation stones for our growth in the future and the growth of the ministry in the months and years ahead. God wrote His truth on our hearts in large letters so that we might share them with others. From that moment forward, we needed to realize the responsibility we had before God as leaders of the next generation of missionaries.

Primarily, we had to lead in focus, in servanthood, in doing what we now knew was necessary to prepare before God for ministry and for battle. Emblazoned on our hearts were the principles of warfare—worship, studying the Word, prayer, and the necessity of consciously surrendering ourselves before God for Him to use us as He sees fit. Our agendas, desires, and fleshly concerns had to be laid aside, allowing Him to stretch us and arrange our priorities.

This final day found us in Pskov, Russia. We had worship time on the bus, diligently waging spiritual battle with every available minute. I asked Sergei to act as my interpreter while I talked with Helena, our translator for the women's parts of the show. She had been our translator for several days, so she knew the show and its message well. I inquired if she would like

to ask Jesus into her heart. Her vital role did not give
her the opportunity to respond during the show, so it
was imperative that we make time then. She said "Yes!"
With a repentant and open heart, she prayed with me
a precious prayer of faith. That night she did the show
as a new babe in Christ. We saw Helena again the next
year and rejoiced to learn that she had shared the gift
of Jesus Christ with many of her friends.

Pskov looked like a war zone. There are people
living on top of people in a city tortured with violence.
Just driving the streets, we could sense communism in
action. Pskov had not yet embraced the reforms of the
Baltic Republics. Statues of Lenin littered the squares.
Lines of people stretched for blocks waiting for alcohol.

Our performance was initiated by a new church,
begun only weeks earlier as an outgrowth of a three-
day crusade by Larry Stockstill from Baton Rouge,
Louisiana. Over one hundred were baptized during the
crusade, and we were invited so that they could "strike
while the iron was hot."

One to two thousand people waited in line over an
hour in the pouring rain for our performance. Since we
were to perform in an amphitheater, we cut the script
so that the people would not have to endure the ele-
ments for another hour-and-a-half. Scott introduced
the show, sharing the complete gospel. During the performance, the rain began coming down in sheets. Um-
brellas shot up, but the terraced seating kept them
from blocking anyone's view. No one made a move to
leave, so we continued the show. Suddenly, the rain
stopped, the skies cleared, and the sun shone brightly.
A rainbow appeared—not one, but two, a double rainbow—a double symbol of God's covenant with the people
on earth. What a blessing for God to move the heavenlies
to shine favor on us!

Hundreds responded to the invitation. Tiger prayed
with the growing crowd, and Zack welcomed them forward to receive a follow-up card, explaining through
Helena that we needed their addresses to send them a
Bible. Within seconds of the translation, the people

mobbed Zack, groping for the cards. Losing his balance, he fell into the crowd and tossed the follow-up cards into the air. Through the clamor, he heard a young girl crying. He sat down on a stool and held her while she cried for she was nearly crushed by the crowd.

The chaos of the moment impressed upon all of us the need to help satisfy their thirst for spiritual truth. The cards were just sheets of paper, but to these desperate people, they were a promise to receive God's lifeline, the Bible. This nation's spiritual thirst must be quenched with the truths of God for if left thirsting, it will be ripe for the counterfeit drenching of Satan.

6

I will go before you and make the rough places smooth; I will shatter the gates of bronze and cut through the iron bars.

(Isa. 45:2)

We hate Christians and Christianity. Even the best of them must be considered our worst enemies. Christian love is an obstacle to the development of the revolution.

(Lunarcharsky, Russian Commissariat of Education)

Establishing Footsteps

I boarded a plane bound for Riga, Latvia, on Sunday, 14 October 1990, only two months after my return from our first venture to the Soviet Union. The purpose of my trip was to discuss the possibilities of two months of ministry in May and August of 1991. The seed sown by the invitation of the Pioneer youth camp director last August and the seeds of love rooted in our hearts for the nation's people were blossoming forth as a passion to return again and again to share the gospel.

We left the Soviet Union last August as changed people. We were no longer American Christians; we were world Christians. John 3:16 does not say, "For God so loved America. . . ." It reads, "For God so loved the world that He gave His only begotten Son. . . ." We witnessed the spiritual hunger of the people. We saw firsthand the hopelessness of their lives—the daily misery. The Soviet Union was a war-torn nation. Its regions may not have seen combat since World War II, but the reigning regime so promulgated its revolutionary ideology and so poisoned the souls of the people that they lived in a constant state of conflict. Nationality warred against nationality, worker against worker, and even brother against brother.

Hatred became a lifestyle, justified by the ideology of the day, its influence so pervasive that few escaped it. Any who doubt the insidious nature of this ideology must look no further than its product, Joseph Stalin, who admitted that his sweetest sleep came after planning the death of an enemy, or read but a few pages from Aleksandr Solzhenitsyn's *Gulag Archipelago*, which details the atrocities committed by those who pledged allegiance to the Soviet flag.

In an effort to survive, "Look out for number one" became the creed of the day, and people lived it with every ounce of strength they could marshal. The only escape they knew came in a bottle, prescribed by the self-serving Soviet regime for all that ails.

The Soviet writer Victor Astafyev wrote in a leading secular Moscow literary magazine: "What happened to us? Who extinguished the light of goodness in our soul? Who blew out the lamp of our conscience . . . ?" In closing his piece, he grieved, "They (Communists) stole it from us and did not give anything in return—giving rise to unbelief, an all-encompassing unbelief. . . . of whom should we ask forgiveness?"

As hopeless as the situation appeared, it was no match for God. We witnessed the transforming power of His love like never before as we shared the simple yet eternal message of His Son's love and sacrifice. The poisoned pen of Marxism held no power as God emblazoned His truths on the hearts of His people. We could do nothing less than return again to satisfy their spiritual hunger. As communism crumbled, the void had to be filled with Christ.

The one-hour flight from Helsinki to Riga carried us over the Baltic Sea. The October sun was setting, and God's handiwork of color and clouds was richly manifest as breathtaking beauty only the Creator could weave. This beauty was a foreshadowing of events to come, for the next thirty-six hours held equally as miraculous evidence of His handiwork and orchestration. To transpire before us were meetings revealing certain "windows of opportunity" that could go down in history as one of the greatest testimonies to the might and power of the One who measures the universe by the span of His hand.

Sergei Shendrick arranged and scheduled our meetings. Sergei was the man who initiated the invitation that secured our visas and passage out of Helsinki last August. A man with a tender heart for his people, he assisted us in entry to many of the Communist youth camps. During our stay, God gave us rich favor with this man. He was not a believer, but he sensed our hearts for the people. Inviting us to return, he expressed his willingness to arrange our ministry for 1991. We gratefully accepted his kind offer.

As we discussed the year ahead, the May trip began to take shape. The thought was that the team would travel to different cities, performing primarily in the theaters. Sergei arranged for us to meet with his boss, Adolfo Sapiro, the director of the Latvian State Youth Theater. God was "establishing footsteps" again, and we gladly moved in wonderment of His hand as it was moving across the hearts and minds of "kings." Sapiro could not have been more receptive when we explained that our mission was to bring the life of Jesus Christ to the Soviet people. He offered any help we needed to accomplish our tasks. It was not until later that we realized the gravity of what God had done. Sergei explained, "Sapiro is very tired. You see, not only is he the director of our theater, but he has an added responsibility as president of the association of all the youth theaters in the entire Soviet Union."

We could not believe the level on which God was moving us into position to minister throughout the entire country, which spans eleven time zones and contains over 110 ethno-linguistic groups. Only His sovereign hand could have linked us with the man who could open any theater venue in the Soviet Union. Meetings with two children's sanatorium directors and the Pioneer youth camp director were abundantly blessed. Each expressed great interest in our teaching their children daily in August. The Vivare sanatorium takes many victims of Chernobyl, the worst nuclear disaster in history. We were equipped like never before to answer the call to "go and make disciples of all nations." Bible Literature International had recently

agreed to provide us with 650 Russian Illustrated Bibles
and 4,500 Russian Illustrated New Testaments.

Who were we that God should open such doors, do
such things, allow us the privilege and blessing to go
into His harvest fields? That question comes to mind as
He continually postures, positions, and prunes in preparation for us to be His vessels. It is humbling to think
He cares so much for all of us that He allows us to
cooperate with His eternal plans to reach out to a lost
and desperate world. What greater joy could we experience than to lay our lives before Him? We are a small
ministry, dwarfed by many, yet used by God. He does
not depend on our resources or limit us because of our
size.

> "Alas, Lord God! Behold, I do not know how to
> speak because I am a youth." But the Lord said to
> me, "Do not say 'I am a youth,' because everywhere
> I send you, you shall go, and all that I command
> you, you shall speak. . . . See, I have appointed you
> this day over the nations and the kingdoms, to
> pluck up and to break down, to destroy and to
> overthrow, to build and to plant." (Jer. 1:6-8, 10)

A meeting with the president of the Latvian
Children's Fund resulted in greater opportunities for
ministry. This group supervises the care of six thousand orphans and five to six thousand disabled children in the republic of Latvia. Disabled youngsters
were hidden from view during the past years of Communist oppression. The Soviet regime disdained any
reminder that human frailties existed in their "uto-
pian" society. These people were kept under lock and
key, receiving only the bare necessities since the Soviets expected no return on their investment.

The May trip unfolded beautifully as Sergei arranged through these meetings for the team to travel
and minister in twelve cities (Moscow, Zagorsk,
Arhangelsk, Slavutich, Chernigov, Vinitsa, Riga,
Daugavpils, Valmiera, Odessa, Ventspils, and Liepaja)
in the three republics of Latvia, the Ukraine, and Russia, taking the gospel into theaters, schools, hospitals,

and even orphanages. As I watched the itineraries develop, I recalled the words of Al Akimoff, International Director of Slavic Ministries. He said, "I believe that the Soviet Union is ripe for the greatest revival and the greatest harvest the world and history has ever seen." This statement from a man with two decades of ministry in Eastern Europe and the U.S.S.R., smuggling Bibles and staying one step ahead of the KGB who sought to seize them.

During our last few minutes in Riga, Sergei and I returned to the hotel room to finalize some details. Exhausted from the arduous schedule of the past thirty-six hours, I knew that one more task lay ahead of me. God sent us on a mission not only to see doors open to hundreds of thousands, but to share heart-to-heart with one man—Sergei.

"Sergei," I began, "I have one more thing I want to talk with you about." Knowing that he had seen *The Greatest Star of All* several times, I shared the gospel with him using those simple illustrations and several key Scriptures. "Sergei, would you like to ask Jesus Christ to come into your life, forgive you of your sins, and take control of your life?"

A pause to reflect. He was a forty-year-old man, his wife an actress and mother of his two children, his face etched with lines furrowed from a hard life under the oppression of communism—the lies, deceit, fear, loneliness, the constant sense that you are just another animal, another number, a meaningless, insignificant human being.

Does life pass before a man like this in an instant, in a pause, in a moment of reflection as the host of heaven seemingly and collectively holds its breath and listens to hear words from his mouth, an answer that would echo a longing, a reaching for the hand of His Creator? God's hand stretches through time and eternity for his, stretching forth from the beginning of the world, through a cross, through an empty tomb.

Did Jesus see this moment as He hung on that cross two thousand years ago? Did He see Sergei? Did

He feel his pain? Was Sergei's agony on the shoulders of the Lamb? As sure as those nails pierced His hands shooting excruciating pain through His body, Jesus saw us in that hotel room. "For the joy set before Him, He endured the cross, despising the shame . . ." (Heb. 12:2).

Sergei's face turned toward me, his tear-glistened eyes met mine. With quiet resolution, he uttered, "Yes, I would like this very much."

Do you hear it? Angels singing, rejoicing in heaven. A collective sigh, a rumbling sound of joy, of exuberance as heaven's host welcomes another prodigal home? Do you see it? The Lamb takes a pen, opens to a new page, and writes carefully and lovingly another name in the Book of Life—Sergei Shendrick.

Do you hear it? A groan, a gasp, an exasperated cry as if from a frothing mouth of a man gone mad . . . cursing, gnashing as another soul slips from the grip of the strongman into the waiting arms of the Savior of the world . . . "He delivered us from the domain of darkness and transferred us to the kingdom of His beloved Son . . ." (Col. 1:13).

Do you see it, the crumbling kingdom? The curtain of darkness retreats, the Light shatters the deep recesses of a man's soul, and He walks out of the pit, throwing off the shackles, the chains, the bonds of the wicked master.

Even as an eye witness, it is difficult to fathom the incredible timing of God and the hunger of the people. We talk about the God-given longing created in every man that cannot be snuffed out, smothered, or destroyed. But to witness it is an extraordinary experience. In America, non-believers have so many movements that fool them into thinking they have satisfied the spiritual void with Satan's spiritual counterfeits. The devil's greatest victory lies in people who encounter him and think they have encountered the one true God.

The Soviet Union is a different story. For over seventy years, the Soviet regime worked to kill the spiritual desires of the people and replace them with communism—an ideology that offered no spiritual pretense. Until recently, these people had no spiritual counterfeits to lull them into a sense of complacency. They recognize their desperate need much more than Americans do because it has not been obscured by spiritual charades. And they embrace the truth wholeheartedly when it is presented.

God heard the cry of the saints within that vast nation's borders. He heard the cry of the saints in other lands crying out for the freedom of their brothers and sisters under the heavy hand of Communism. And now He answers them, in the fullness of time. No one can deny God's hand upon that nation. A revolution thunders—a revolution of the heart.

7

Then you, my people, will know that I am the Lord, when I open your graves and bring you up from them. I will put my Spirit in you and you will live, and I will settle you in your own land.

(Ezek. 37:13-14)

Transforming a Nation—One Life at a Time

Ezekiel 37 speaks of the transforming power of God. The Spirit of the Lord sets Ezekiel in the middle of a valley—a valley full of bones. God led him back and forth among the bones and said, "Son of man, can these bones live?" Ezekiel replied, "O Sovereign Lord, you alone know." Then the Lord commanded,

Prophesy to these bones and say to them, "Dry bones, hear the word of the Lord! This is what the Sovereign Lord says to these bones: 'I will make breath enter you, and you will come to life. . . . Then you will know that I am the Lord.'" As he prophesied, Ezekiel heard the sound of bones rattling, saw tendons and flesh appear on them, and skin cover them. But there was no breath. Again, the Lord commanded him to prophesy, "Come from the four winds, O breath, and breathe into these slain, that they may live." When he prophesied as the Lord commanded, breath entered them and they rose up forming a vast army. The Lord spoke, "Son of man, these bones are the whole house of Israel. They say, 'Our bones are dried up and our hope is gone; we are cut off.'" Once again, He commanded Ezekiel to prophesy, "This is what the Sovereign Lord says: 'O my people, I am going to open your graves and bring you up from them . . . Then you, my people will know that I am the Lord, when

I open your graves and bring you up from them. I
will put my Spirit in you and you will live, and I
will settle you in your own land. Then you will
know that I the Lord have spoken, and I have done
it, declares the Lord.'"

Vadim was a young Russian the team met in
Jurmala. In a cynical tone, he questioned Scott, "Do
you believe what you do makes a difference?"

"Of course I do," Scott replied. "Why would I have
come so far to do it?"

This young Russian studied Scott, somewhat puzzled
at his resolute response. "I believe Russia is a damned
country. God has damned our country. Why else could
we have such evils?"

Vadim felt like the people of Israel, cut off and
hopeless. "What is this Jesus? Jesus cannot do anything. These children just hear the words and come
forward. They are not really making a decision. If I
accept Christ, it will not make any difference. I still
will not have much to eat."

His circumstances had calloused him, but he would
still come around to talk. Vadim was searching, yet
afraid to believe. The Soviet legacy of deceit, the lies,
the broken promises still held him captive. Would he
ever be able to trust again? Was his thinking typical of
most intellectuals?

Many may share Vadim's feelings of hopelessness
and isolation, but they are not out of God's reach. Like
Ezekiel, we are privileged to witness God breathing life
into the people of the Soviet Union. This vast nation's
people were despairing and isolated, but God, in His
infinite mercy, is transforming their existence from
death to life and settling them in their own land.

We see it at every performance. Children and adults
alike enter the auditorium desperate people, yearning
for freedom from their hopeless existence. They enter
dry bones, but they leave alive with the Spirit of God.
God is transforming this nation—one life at a time. It is
the unseen weaving of a new fabric that takes time,
diligence, and perseverance. When we fully embrace

God's call to "go and make disciples," we are surrendering to and undertaking the task of pouring our lives into others. It takes time, lots of it.

Little Katya, who watched the performance in August 1990 from her father's shoulders, tugged on Tiger's tail. Sonia turned around, recognizing those big brown eyes immediately. Her mother followed, and then her father. His moustache looked just as thick the year before, but this time it topped a radiant smile. Anxious to communicate, he said in broken English, "What you told our family last year has made such a difference in our lives . . . thank you!" Katya clung to her Bible, and he held the follow-up letter.

We saw them again in August at a Pioneer camp. They shared with us about how they read the Bible, pray, and attend church. They may not yet have fully understood the power of the Holy Spirit to give new life, but they knew where their strength lay in the midst of chaos. "You brought God to our lives and our lives have changed because of what you've done."

In observing this family and the healing in their hearts, we were reminded of Malachi 4:6, which reads, "He will turn the hearts of the fathers to their children, and the hearts of the children to their fathers. . . ." God truly blessed each of us by allowing a glimpse at Katya and her family three different times. It is amazing to see what He can do through the faith of a child and the reading of His Word.

Periodically, we do have the opportunity to follow a Katya and watch God use the surrendered heart of a child. It is indeed a special blessing. Through our eyes of faith, we see each new creature leaving our performances committed to sharing the love of Christ. We see each one touching lives.

After the first of two shows in a theater in Zeleningrad, Suzie (Bear) noticed a woman writing a message in English on the back of her follow-up card. When she completed it, she handed it to Suzie. The message read, "If it possible, send us one Bible especially for children. Thank you! Olga." She explained

that she had two daughters, Kate and Ann, who also
accepted Christ that day. She related God's touch on
her life and the lives of her girls. The back of her girls'
response cards revealed a similar request: "My sister
and I dream to get Bible for children and our mother
will read it to us every evening before sleeping. If
possible, send us one Bible especially for children. Thank
you."

Suzie asked Olga to wait until the crowd of children
dispersed. As the auditorium cleared, they went backstage and Suzie gave her a children's Bible. We wish
we could have given a Bible to each child, but we could
only raise enough funds for five hundred Russian
Children's Bibles. The team had to be very prayerful
and selective in their distribution. Olga was truly overcome with appreciation and shared that she would
read to her daughters every day so that they could
learn more about Jesus.

After the second show, Suzie felt a jerk on her
costume. She turned around to find Olga beaming from
ear to ear. "I took the Bible home, and during lunch,
my children begged me to read it. I just wanted to
thank you again for giving us the Bible." Oh, that every
American could witness the excitement of these people,
adults and children alike, over the Bible. Such conviction mounts in your soul as their joy confronts you with
your tendency to take the Word of God for granted.

Lilly, a woman who looked to be in her mid-sixties,
was a balcony attendant for the Latvian State Youth
Theater. When Brenda entered the balcony to hand out
follow-up cards after the first of eighteen performances
in that theater, Lilly requested a card and told Brenda
that she had asked Jesus into her heart that day. The
childish costumes and the frivolity of the musical did
not prevent this older woman from hearing its eternal
message. Brenda continued to go to the balcony after
each show to hand out cards. Lilly knew when it was
time for her to arrive and always greeted her with a
smile and a hug. Her appreciation for the team's bringing the message of Jesus showed in her expression and
in her embrace.

One day, Lilly was more excited to see Brenda than usual. She had some news. Two of her grandchildren had attended the performance and asked Jesus into their hearts. What a blessing to see the joy of this grandmother as she told of the newfound faith of her precious grandchildren. "For I will pour water upon him that is thirsty, and floods upon the dry ground: I will pour my spirit upon thy seed, and my blessing upon thine offspring" (Isa. 44:3).

Debbie was mobbed as she attempted to hand out response cards after a performance. Working her way through the crowd, she noticed the theater director holding out his hand to receive a card. Curious about whether it was for him, she inquired, "For you?" He smiled and nodded, but a nod and smile are standard procedure even in the absence of understanding. After the confusion subsided, Debbie grabbed Anna the translator to find out for sure whether he asked Jesus into his heart. He responded, "Yes!" It was indeed a joy to see God use a children's production to touch the heart of a theater professional.

Little did we know that two other theater professionals would join our ministry as a result of the May trip. On 3 July 1992, Tatiana Larchenko, eighteen, and Inna Kosheleva, twenty-four, joined our teams in Discipleship Rehearsal Camp as new members. These two Russian-trained actresses were working as part of the Russian Theater Troupe in residence at the Latvian State Youth Theater. Each saw *The Greatest Star of All* in May 1991 and responded to the invitation to ask Jesus into their hearts. Now, they desire to use their talents to have an impact on the children of their world. In the city of Novostroyka, the team performed before many people who had never seen Americans. During the finale, one small boy left his seat and walked the long aisle to the stage. He stood with his eyes focused on the team, longing to be near them. Nothing seemed unnatural about his response. In fact, it was the most natural and fitting of responses. Jesus was drawing him into His kingdom, and he was responding with an

open and obedient heart. At the invitation hundreds
joined him at the front, all seeking "the greatest star of
all." But that boy is locked in our memories as a lamb
who waited for nothing when Jesus, the good shep-
herd, called.

While Sonia was handing out follow-up cards after
one performance, she spotted a fourteen-year-old with
his hand raised. Touched by the courage of this young
teen, she asked him if he had a Bible. He shook his
head and said, "No." Sonia hurried backstage to get a
Bible, and she handed it to him. He looked confused
but finally realized that it was a gift. Through Anna,
he asked, "Is this the book I can read to learn how to
live my life?" Through her tears, Sonia nodded, "Yes!"
What faith! As he walked away leafing through the
pages, he looked at it in disbelief. In his hands, he held
the answers and the strength for the obstacles and
uncertainties life hurled at him. This was one young
man who would search for truth as silver and gold.

Since our first trip to this land, this people's handling of God's Word has challenged and inspired me.
They treat it, appropriately, as the most priceless treasure on earth. Ena and her two daughters, Nellie and
Nina, each handed their response cards to Sonia, sharing with her that they had all given their lives to
Christ. Their hearts yearned to learn more about their
Savior, and Ena asked where she could find more to
teach her children. Sonia gave them two Bibles, one for
the girls and one for mom. Accepting their gifts, Ena
declared, "We will read and learn more about Jesus
every day . . . we love you . . . thank you!" Ena and her
precious daughters were three of 309 "treasures" who
gave their hearts to Christ that day.

Marchello was one of the team's translators for the
May trip. He was twenty years old and attended the
University of Moscow. A school vacation freed him to
translate for the team. He traveled with them, translated the show, observed them during worship, and
talked with the team members about Christ. Brandon
shared the gospel with him at length one night, and

Brenda talked with him about Christ at every opportunity. During one conversation with Brenda, he said, "You say the show is for children. But I'm embarrassed because I have never heard these things."

On his last day with the team, Brenda felt an urgency to ask him his decision about Christ. As she was praying and reading Jeremiah, this verse leaped out at her, "Today, I have put my words in your heart." She prayed for the chance to speak with him.

At the end of the show, God provided the opportunity for her to talk with Marchello. In the midst of the demanding atmosphere that customarily follows a performance, she found herself sitting at the end of the stage with him. They chatted about his trip home, and then she said, "Well, Marchello, are you ready to meet the greatest star of all?" Without hesitation, he responded, "Yes!" They left the crowds of people running to see the team members and walked over to an open window. Nothing was to interrupt this very important exchange. There Marchello asked Jesus Christ into his heart. The following day, he returned to school, to the same schedule and the same studies. However, Marchello's life would never be the same again. That day, he became a new creation. "Therefore if any man be in Christ, he is a new creature; old things are passed away; behold, all things are become new" (2 Cor. 5:17).

The physical and spiritual labor of these trips is exhausting. Each night we return to the hotel tempted to eat and go right to bed. But we learned in Helsinki to be ready for whatever God requires. We are His vessels, and our comfort is not our primary concern.

One particular night in Daugavpils, Latvia, Sergei scheduled a meeting between the team and some theater students who had seen the show. After two performances, the team was less than enthusiastic about the thought of a cultural exchange. A few of our team members have theater backgrounds, but some do not, so they were equally as anxious about their ability to make a meaningful contribution to this type of discussion. However, they attended the meeting, ready for whatever God required of them.

Many of the Latvian students attended. Americans are an attraction for the young people, especially Americans in the same field.

The evening crawled as they drank strong coffee and ate pastries. The leader of their group gave an introductory speech. He welcomed the team and just as they expected, he mentioned their interest in the cultural aspects of our work. As he finished his remarks, Scott, the Red Team leader, stood to speak. He explained that yes, we were performers, but our reason for performing was very different from theirs. We were in their country because of our love for Jesus Christ. He was the reason we did what we did.

Scott's remarks altered the course of the evening. The theater students grew more comfortable, and the atmosphere became more casual. Two of the more rambunctious students got a guitar and began to share folk songs. The team shared upbeat Christian songs. Soon, these new friends were snake dancing, moon-walking, and the team broke down and shared the Red Team food rap. Song after song was exchanged with members from both groups sharing creatively and freely.

During the final parlay, the team shared Michael W. Smith's "Friends," and the Latvians shared a sad but true story of a Russian who fell in love with the governor of California's daughter. He was Orthodox, and in order to marry her, he had to return to Russia for permission. He traveled back to his native land via Alaska and while in Siberia, caught a fatal cold. The song's chorus was "I love you, though I'll never see you again."

Finally, Scott recognized an opportunity to raise this evening above a cultural exchange. Through Anna, he told them that the two groups need not be separated permanently. Accepting Jesus into their hearts would ensure their spending eternity together.

With that, the team rose to begin their good-byes. The students stopped them. One walked over to Anna and asked her to translate. He said, "We want you to teach us how to pray."

Scott's initial reaction was "Wow, what an opportunity to teach these actors about prayer!" A team member nudged him and said, "Go for it, Griz. They want to pray and they said, 'You know, like at the end of the show.'" Scott then understood the significance and depth of their question.

What an overwhelming experience for this team. All thirty-three of those students wanted to pray the prayer of repentance and ask Christ into their hearts. Scott directed Anna to translate word for word. He walked them through the Gospel, stressing that this was a commitment. Again, he queried, "Are you sure about this?" Not one declined.

Scott led them through a prayer that only the Holy Spirit could craft. Not one of those students could have prayed that prayer without recognizing the earnest commitment involved. In a few precious moments, thirty-three individuals passed from death into life as they prayed with Scott, asking Christ to reign in their lives.

Good-byes took much longer. Some of the students were overwhelmed with emotion as they said their farewells. Something had been deposited in their hearts—something that words could not express. No longer were they merely fellow performers. Jesus bridged the gap, and they parted new brothers and sisters in Christ. God turned a cultural exchange into yet another glimpse at a nation transformed.

Unfortunately, there is a bitter aspect to taking part in this revolution of the heart. It is the painful sorrow of sharing with someone who cannot bring himself to leave the past behind and follow Christ. Something still holds them captive. They listen to our message, but they cannot let go and cleave to Christ. The desperate struggle with bondage moves us deeply each time we witness it. We pray for their freedom.

Andre watched from a distance as Brenda attempted to talk with some children after the show. Finally, he walked over, told her that he spoke some English, and offered to help her communicate.

As the children began to disperse, he asked some questions about the Lord. Since communication of any depth was difficult, she grabbed her Bible hoping to find a verse or verses that he could understand. As she thumbed through the pages, he asked her what she held in her hand. When she responded that it was her Bible, the look on his face broke her heart. Andre was nearly twenty years old, and he had never seen a Bible.

"Can I hold your Bible and look at it?" he asked. She handed it to him, and he looked for a moment with the awe that the Word of God should inspire. Carefully, he laid it back in her hands.

Andre was hungry to hear about Jesus, but they did not seem able to penetrate the language barrier. The Scriptures she found were too hard for him to understand. Brenda breathed a prayer and began again, picking and choosing each word carefully. Through God's grace, he finally understood. She gave him a Russian Bible of his very own.

Andre did not give his heart to Jesus at that moment, but his eyes welled with tears as he accepted the gift of God's Word. He heard the gospel, and he could read it again and again. When we think of Andre, we rest in the sufficiency of God's Word to nurture the seed planted in his heart that day.

One of our translators was another who gripped our hearts with her inability to give her life to Christ. Luda was trying to survive while caring for a severely retarded ten-year-old daughter alone. Her husband walked out on her after the birth of a less-than-perfect daughter. She was very interested in spiritual things, searching for answers and the strength to endure such hardship.

The team prayed with her about her problems, talked with her about Jesus, and Scott shared with her at length in response to a question she asked about hearing and understanding the Holy Spirit. It was tragic, but she could not bring herself to trust Christ and lay her burdens down at the foot of the cross. May God break down the wall that separates her from His loving embrace.

Ahgpelo was a young man who befriended Sue after one performance. She walked out after the show, and he gave her two pins, one with a picture of the Kremlin and another with a picture of a government building. He handed her a follow-up card, and she inquired as to whether he asked Jesus into his heart. *"Da!"* he replied. She asked if he had a Bible. "No," he responded. Sue hurried backstage, found one, and handed it to him. He took the Bible with great excitement.

After the second show, Sue walked off-stage as usual to pray. Ahgpelo waited for her with a book. A short time later, they stole a chance to talk. He was seventeen and at eighteen would be going into the Red Army. For that reason, he could not "have Jesus right now." The language barrier kept Sue from getting the full story, but we can guess that Ahgpelo knew only too well what he would undoubtedly encounter attempting to live the Christian faith while filling his place in the ranks of the Red Army. Ahgpelo was yet another soul enslaved by his service to the Marxist regime. He may have served for a little while before the dissolution of the troops, but we rejoice that now he is free to serve Christ. As with all the people of the Commonwealth, we pray that he richly invests his freedom in godly pursuits.

Andrew was a fourth grader in a Moscow primary school. I visited his classroom during one of our advance trips. Lenny LeBlanc accompanied me and performed some songs for the children. Andrew was obviously angered at our presence and the messages of the songs. When I began to share the gospel with the children (something I would not be permitted to do in the public schools of America), his temper flared. At the invitation to accept Christ, every child stood except Andrew. His eyes were filled with animosity. When I asked our translator about him, she explained that his parents were committed Communists. They wasted no

time in poisoning their child with the prescribed atheistic propaganda. And at age nine, their lies were firmly
rooted in his heart.

I approached him and shook his hand, but his expression never softened. Our belief in Christ rendered
us enemies in his eyes. As we shared with the children
and took pictures, Andrew grew so disturbed that he
bolted from the room shouting, "I am getting out of
here. I do not want to listen to anymore of this."

We pray for Andrew and others like him who at
such a tender age harbor such hatred in their hearts.
We pray for their freedom from the bondage of Marxism. The wickedness of seventy years built walls, hard-
ened hearts, and chilled the very blood that runs
through men's veins. But we know that it is not "a
battle against flesh and blood, but against the rulers,
against the powers, against the world forces of this
darkness, against the spiritual forces of wickedness in
the heavenly places" (Eph. 6:12).

I believe that the first two-thirds of ministry is, of
necessity, warfare—spiritual warfare. The hard heart
of an Andrew cannot be softened with arguments or
words. Through intercession, worship, going before the
throne and speaking Andrew's name before the Father,
the Spirit can melt his hard exterior, tearing down the
walls brick by brick, preparing the way for the seed of
His Word to be sown in tilled soil.

God told Jeremiah, "I have appointed you this day
over the nations and over the kingdoms, to pluck up
and to break down, to destroy and to overthrow, to
build and to plant" (Jer. 1:10). The first two-thirds of
ministry, the plucking up, breaking down, destroying
and overthrowing, is the battle in the heavenlies, setting the stage for the physical ministry of building and
planting. Without this preparation, we are merely
"showing up," and the presence and ministry of God
cannot go forth in the power and depth He desires.

Paul wrote to the Corinthian church, "For though
we walk in the flesh, we do not war according to the
flesh, but the weapons of our warfare are not of the

flesh, but divinely powerful for the destruction of fortresses" (2 Cor. 10:3-4). I am convinced and believe with all my heart that the incredible results we see only happen because the battle has been fought and won in the Spirit. Thus, the case is not closed on an Andre, Ahgpelo, or an Andrew as we continue to fight for their lives on our knees, hoping that one day they will worship with us around God's throne.

> After these things I looked, and behold, a great multitude, which no one could count, from every nation and all tribes and peoples and tongues, standing before the throne and before the Lamb, clothed in white robes, and palm branches were in their hands; and they cried out with a loud voice saying, "Salvation to our God who sits on the throne, and to the Lamb." And all the angels were standing around the throne and around the elders and the four living creatures and they fell on their faces before the throne and worshiped God, saying, "Amen, blessing and glory and wisdom and thanksgiving and honor and power and might, be to our God forever and ever. Amen." (Rev. 7:9-12).

8

Strengthen the feeble hands, steady the knees that give way; say to those fearful hearts, "Be strong, do not fear; your God will come . . . He will come to save you."

(Isa. 35:3-4)

The Forgotten Children

Ministering in the children's hospitals of the Commonwealth offers a new, more graphic encounter with a philosophy that puts no value on human life apart from its utility. In three years, we have toured and ministered in many hospitals, but we have never gotten over the shock. The nauseating smell of insidious disease lingers in every hallway. Plaster peels off walls that have not had a new coat of paint in decades. The floors are filthy, and cats roam unencumbered.

Space is limited, so children are packed into small ten-by-twelve rooms, six beds in a room. They receive very little personal attention because nursing staff is in such short supply. In many cases, one or two nurses attend an entire floor with perhaps eight to ten rooms. If it were not for the mothers who attend to their children every day, care would be painfully insufficient.

Antibiotics and pain relievers are scarce and children's vitamins a luxury. Parents have never heard of Reye Syndrome, so they think nothing of giving their youngsters aspirin. Very few hospitals have any diagnostic equipment, and if they do, it is frequently of the World War II era. The best children's orthopedic hospital in Moscow and perhaps the entire Commonwealth still uses a 1941 X-ray machine.

Illnesses rarely see a cure. Medical expertise and technology trails that of the United States by generations. Treatment is primitive at best. Many of the children lying in their beds with little hope of recovery suffer from illnesses in which treatment is considered little more than routine in America. One frequent sight in the orthopedic hospitals is children with both legs casted and spread apart with a hockey stick taped between them. This is the standard treatment for congenital hip displacia. If the problem is diagnosed at a young age, there is some hope that this archaic method can improve the child's condition. However, the older children will probably never fully recover. In many cases, they are victims of misdiagnoses from hospitals in other Republics.

Victims of paralysis are condemned to live lives of isolation. No provisions were made for their comfort in a society that considers them nothing more than a liability. Families cannot afford the expense of caring for them so many will not know life outside an institution. Lying flat on their backs in a bed looking at four gray walls is the only existence they will know.

Julia asked to see "the bear." Suzie walked over to a little girl lying on a table and sat down beside her. She was paralyzed below the waist. Julia looked up and smiled as she told Bear that she asked Jesus to forgive her sins and come into her heart during our outreach there. Her brown eyes radiated a light that only the Savior gives. Suzie caressed her hands. What will become of this precious little girl? The hospital can do nothing for her, yet there she stays. She and so many others like her are captives of bodies that are nothing more than shells. Unless conditions improve drastically in the next few years, many of these children will never learn to read or write. They will be totally dependent on their caretakers. Mainstreaming the disabled is an alien concept. Attempting to alleviate the suffering by helping these children lead normal lives was not a priority of the Soviets.

Suzie watched as the nurse picked Julia up and placed her over her shoulder like a limp rag doll. Julia's physical condition had not changed, but she now knew that Jesus Christ cared for her and lived in her heart.

Her smile was proof positive that He had revealed His love for her in a special way. She continued to wave as she rounded the corner, carried out of sight.

After the shows, the team members usually stay in costume and tour some of the floors with the children too sick to attend. Walking the dimly lit hallways, the cast tries to bring some color and joy to lives of patients who must live in such intolerable conditions. The children lie in their beds and study the team. They receive very few visitors; so to see animals, Zack, and the clowns, is an adventure.

In many of the hospitals, mothers will tend to their children due to the shortage of nursing staff. We watched these anguished parents as they studied a child wondering about his future. Would he get better or would his condition deteriorate? One father rubbed the shaved head of his son as if tormented by thoughts of the future. A child's condition holds the whole family captive.

A little orphan boy in the Moscow orthopedic hospital brought home the devastating reality of day to day existence in isolation. He was orphaned at birth. Blind and crippled, he could not move from his crib. We watched as he rocked back and forth—a common symptom for children his age who receive no attention or affection. This little one had nothing to fill his day but his rocking. The nurses had no time to hold him. Other children lay in their beds, watching the activity around them. His blindness locked him away from the world around him. Day after day, he sat in his crib and rocked, yearning for a touch, some contact with the world that passed him by. He did not cry. He uttered not a sound. The rhythmic rocking was his only scream— a scream that welled up deep within him, yet had no voice. A touch stopped the rocking, but it was only a brief reprieve. A bottle or a quick check do little to relieve the pain of loneliness.

Where were his parents? Did they think of him often? Were they simply not able to cope with his disability, or did their philosophy of life bar them from giving love to a babe who was less than perfect?

A picture of "Grandfather Lenin" hung in the hallway outside his room. Should this little one have thanked the man who propagated a philosophy that considers him a liability? Should he have thanked him for his wonderful childhood?

Groups of girls and boys approached the team members after the show just to talk for a little while. Severed from their families due to illness, these children have little opportunity to ask questions of an adult who cares for them and will take the time to lovingly respond. The teams radiate love, and they recognize their sincerity. The Holy Spirit blesses the time, knitting hearts together so that the team is able to minister to their needs.

Suzie was inundated with questions about the musical, God, and America. As Scott and Brandon fielded some questions, one fourteen-year-old boy piped up, "Where can we get some Bibles?" These children desperately longed to know Jesus in an intimate way. How many American teen-agers demonstrate such excitement about the Word of God?

During final tear down, the team noticed some boys watching them. Eyes pinned on the stage, they inched closer and closer to the prop box, curious about its contents. Before long, they were into the props, wearing the hats and blowing the horn. Their dirty fingers left smudges all over our equipment, but the smudges mattered little when we saw the smiles on their faces.

Crowded into ten-by-twelve rooms, there is very little room for them to play. Toys are a luxury most do not enjoy. They spend their time lying or sitting in bed. Our prop box offered the "dirt boys" a short hiatus from the monotony.

Chernobyl, the 1986 nuclear disaster that the Kremlin grudgingly announced three days after the insidious fumes exploded into the atmosphere, victimized tens of thousands of the nation's children. They suffer from blood disorders, bone diseases, many forms of cancer, and genetic defects thanks to the government's reckless disregard for the populace. We perform before

many children suffering the consequences of Chernobyl.
They appear normal on the outside, but their bodies
are ravaged by debilitating disease. When I asked one
doctor about the devastating effects of Chernobyl, he
said, "Don't talk to me about Chernobyl. There are
chernobyls all over this land." Thanks to Sweden,
Chernobyl was discovered and captured the world's
attention, but for decades the government had been
dumping radioactive nuclear waste into rivers and lakes
throughout the Soviet Union with absolutely no regard
for its devastating effect on millions of lives.

Agnese wanted to see us. She was bedridden, paralyzed from the neck down from two spinal injuries. Her
room in the corner of the seventh floor was the only
home she had known for two years. Her respirator was
her only link with life. Three animals, a clown, Zack,
Barry, and I filed into the room as a gaunt, cheek-
sunken face managed a smile. The respirator hissed,
its ominous rhythm a constant reminder of the fine
line between life and death.

The doctor told us that Agnese had no hope. The
translator said that she was at the mercy of her parents' decision since the doctors had given up on her.

Agnese shook every hand, paw, and clown glove
that reached out to her. She reached out and touched
our hearts. The smile faded as if the effort to turn the
corners of her frail mouth up took an incredible amount
of energy away from an already drained body.

"Tish," I asked, "You're closest. Would you please
pray for Agnese?" Words of hope. Words of healing. His
presence filled the room. Tears filled my eyes. I handed
Agnese a tract. She stared at the picture. I got a promise that someone would read it to her. My prayer is
that the prayer of commitment will become hers.

The Red Team met Nina Korddadde while performing in the town of Touriste. She suffered from curvature of the spine. We received the following letter from
her. Nina's cry for help typifies the desperate cry of
thousands.

Thank you for everything, especially that I could
attend your play. I really like it. You'll have to
excuse me, but I am unable to write in English, so
I will write in Russian. Our family is well. Only I
don't have parents to raise me, but our aunt who is
our guardian is raising us. Why us? Because there
are three of us. I have two brothers; Pera and
Zurab and I am Nina. Our parents gave us up
because they did not want us. I prayed to God for
an aunt to take us. And what happened? God heard
me. Why am I in the hospital? Because I have
curvature of the spine. I try to straighten it but it
is of no use. Every day I pray to God for Him to
help me. Can you help me, friend? What am I to do?
I want to ask you for help. CAN YOU HELP ME?
I was born in Georgia. My father is Georgian and
mother is Russian, and I am a half-breed mixture
of Georgian and Russian. I was born November 4,
1974. I am 16. When I came to your play and
started to watch it, then I felt, this is it, HAPPI-
NESS! I never in my life felt like that. Then we all
knelt to pray. Yes, a few laughed, but they didn't
understand. This was very serious when you prayed,
and that you must believe in God is most serious.
Thank you, friend, for everything, thank you for
visiting the Soviet Union, thank you for visiting
our hospital.

A letter like this one grips your heart with the need
to bring the light of Jesus into their dark, hopeless
worlds. Both in November 1991 and May 1992, I inquired about Nina's whereabouts when we revisited
the Moscow Children's Hospital to deliver medical supplies and plan future ministry. Both times, my inquiries were to no avail. However, a short stopover in
Moscow with the Blue Team on 24 June 1992 on the
way to the Black Sea area brought a wonderful surprise. As Sergei greeted us, he said, "Greg, meet Nina
Korddadde." There stood a beautiful young girl smiling
brightly, with her big brown eyes gleaming. Neither
the team nor I could believe our eyes or contain our
excitement. Sergei had not given up the search and
had found Nina in this city of ten million. He readily

admitted, "God helped me find her." Our hope is to bring her to America soon for the medical help she so desperately needs.

During my first visit to a hospital, God planted the seed in my heart to begin exploring the possibility of serving as a conduit in getting medical supplies to these hospitals. How can we witness such need and not do something? Since that time, we have given hundreds of pounds of supplies to different hospitals and sanatoriums. Amazingly, all were grateful for the help, but they echo the same refrain: "We can make do with scarce supplies. We always have. The one thing that the children desperately need that we cannot provide are performances." They cannot provide the joy, the color, or particularly the happiness that Nina Korddadde speaks of in her letter.

During our June 1992 trip, the director of the Sochi Children's Hospital gathered us in his office to express his thanks for our ministry there. As Dan Eaddy, the Blue Team, and myself entered, his comments began, "We receive humanitarian aid from time to time for which we are grateful, but what you have given our children is your hearts, and from your hearts. You brought something better than medicine—joy—and I am afraid it has been so effective that we may not have any patients left on Monday."

These children need someone who cares for them when they are separated from their parents for great lengths of time or abandoned by parents who could not cope. Christ's love relieves the day to day misery. He is the only one who can truly comfort them, and we are privileged to see Him extend that comfort in unique ways. As I think of what God can do in the lives of these children, I am reminded of Isaiah 35, which reads:

> Strengthen the feeble hands, steady the knees that give way; say to those fearful hearts, "Be strong, do not fear; your God will come, he will come with vengeance; with divine retribution he will come to save you." Then will the eyes of the blind be opened and the ears of the deaf unstopped. Then will the

lame leap like a deer, and the mute tongue shout
for joy. . . . They will enter Zion with singing;
everlasting joy will crown their heads. Gladness
and joy will overtake them, and sorrow and sighing
will flee away.

We are truly honored to be used by Jesus in ministering to these children. And we are humbled to think
that He allows us to provide them comfort and solace
in the midst of their anguish. Caring and comforting
"the least of these" is a blessing beyond measure. You
always leave wishing you could do more.

9

You will call a nation you do not know and a nation which knows you not will run to you, because of the Lord your God.

(Isa. 55:5)

Discipling a Generation

Jesus said, "Go and make disciples of all nations. . . ." That is His mandate. He did not say, "Go and make converts." Please understand that I believe evangelism is extremely important. I am not minimizing it in the least. However, as our understanding of Christ's mandate grew, we recognized that August 1991 held much greater potential in this revolution of the heart than any other trip. Not only would we have the opportunity to evangelize, but the Pioneer camp directors' invitations also offered us time to share crucial foundational principles of the Christian faith. Jesus does not call us to birth babes with no thought to their nurture. He calls us to care for these new babes in Christ, responsibly seeing that they grow in their newfound faith.

Of course, questions surfaced. It is a tremendous responsibility to teach these children about Christ and their identity in Him. As one camp director said, "These children are blank slates." Great care had to be taken to ensure that we were sharing pure biblical truth, not truth tainted by our culture. Could we develop teaching that would successfully minister and take root in these youth, transcending the cultural, political, and language barriers? Could we see a generation raised forth that would lead others to Him?

As we prayed, God gave us vision for spinning our lessons off of the GROW principle in our sequel musical, *Never Be the Same*. We developed six one-hour sessions. For the first lesson the team performed *The Greatest Star of All* to present the gospel. The performance was followed by questions about the show and an invitation. We closed by distributing Bibles. Every child we encountered with a smile or hug received his own Russian Illustrated Children's New Testament graciously provided by Bible Literature International. Before they departed the auditorium, we gave them their first reading assignment. By the end of our discipleship time together, they had read completely through their New Testaments. Assignments aside, parents later told me that their children read through the entire book in one day!

The next four lessons shared each letter of GROW: G—Go to God in prayer; R—Read God's Word; O—Obey God's Word; and W—Witness. I provided the team members with an outline of what needed to be accomplished in each of these sessions. Two team members were assigned to each letter. They were given creative freedom and the responsibility to decide the Scripture references and develop a skit and teaching material that would include the entire team. They also had to select memory verses that shared the concepts.

For instance, Scott and Sonia were assigned the letter *W*—Witness. They did a skit based on Acts 16, the chapter in which Paul and Silas witnessed even after they were thrown in jail. The children all joined in the song and performed the sound effects for the earthquake. Scott had a friend (puppet) named "Wally Witness" who taught the children the memory verse Mark 16:15.

They used "The Grow Show," a take-off on "Family Feud" and "Jeopardy," to review the other three letters. Brenda won the grand prize: "Riches in Heaven." These lessons were fun for us, but our greatest pleasure was the eternal impressions made on the children.

The final session included the performance of our sequel musical, *Never Be the Same,* which carries a strong discipleship message and shares the GROW principle throughout. This musical cemented the principles in their minds and hearts.

The children's ability to grasp the lessons amazed us. They listened attentively, answered the questions, and completed their homework faithfully. Wherever we ventured in the camps, we saw children propped against trees, sitting on benches, in window sills, lying in the grass, all reading their Bibles. They were beginning to realize that the Bible was a book that would literally change their lives. The Bibles became their "most prized possession." At one camp, we were literally stampeded when we began to distribute the Bibles. Imagine Satan's outrage at these children's enthusiasm about studying the Bible in camps originally designed to indoctrinate in the atheistic tenets of Marxism. A revolution of powerful proportions stirred this nation as children from all over the Soviet Union, from the Republics of Russia, Latvia, Belorussia, the Ukraine, and even Armenia, heard the "good news" of Christ and were nurtured in the Christian faith.

Ending each session with a Bible reading assignment and beginning the next with a review encouraged them in their study of the Word. During the review, I would ask, "Who can come up and share on the microphone what they learned?" And hands would shoot up all over the auditorium. The answers were not one or two word phrases as you might expect. They had the pertinent Scriptures memorized. These children absorbed the teachings and the Scriptures like dry sponges. They thirsted for spiritual truth and they recognized the ability of the Word to quench that thirst.

We asked a question about Jesus, and in a matter of moments, we heard His life story repeated as it appears in the Bible. It was staggering to witness the Holy Spirit working in their lives and lending His power to the lessons. They demonstrated such understanding; no other explanation was plausible. Virtually since birth these children were taught to believe that the content of our lessons was absolute nonsense, that communism was the only hope for the future. Yet the minute we began to speak truth, they recognized it as just that—truth. They cast all the years of indoctrination aside for what we offered. Two years earlier in these same camps and in their schools, these children sat through lessons on Marxism, Lenin, and the future of communism.

In August 1991, they were learning about prayer, reading God's Word, obeying God, and sharing their faith. At the end of our lessons, every child could explain each letter of the GROW principle and quote the corresponding verse. All our doubts about discipling these children vanished in the face of God's power. At Yuri Gagarian camp, Suzie spied a little seven-year-old in the back of the auditorium who would begin to raise his hand in response to a question and then hesitate. It was obvious that he knew the answer, but he was shy about participating. Offering a little encouragement, Suzie tapped him on the shoulder and motioned for him to go ahead and raise his hand. When he did, I immediately called on him. Down he came to the microphone, and from that time forward, his little cap popped up in the back every time a question was asked. He never gave an incorrect answer. I dubbed him "Billy Grahamsky." Toward the end of our time together, I asked him privately what he wanted to be when he grew up. In his words, he wants to be a "church worker." Watch out, Reverend Graham.

The children's hunger grew with each lesson. I spotted a gentleman I had met earlier named Sergei Skvortsov. He was escorting his daughter to our next GROW lesson at the Gagarian camp. Sergei and his family lived in Moscow where he worked as an Emmy award-winning producer for Russian State Television. "It's good to see you again," I said. He replied, "This is really something. We told the children that they could either go play and swim at the beach or come to the spiritual lesson, but they couldn't do both. They chose the lesson."

Vacationing with Sergei were several other families. One mother pointed to her daughter walking in the distance and said, "She has read that Bible since the moment you gave it to her. She wants to do nothing else."

Another amazing aspect of this ministry was to see the children apply what they learned. In America, we learn a new biblical principle, but invariably do not apply it because of some inhibition or doubt. These children harbored no inhibitions or doubts. We taught that you could go to God in prayer about anything. And that is just what they did. We saw the child-like faith that Jesus talked about—not childish, but child-like faith.

At one camp, the children talked all afternoon and into the evening about what they learned after our morning performance. Even after the children went to bed, the counselors stayed up until 3:00 A.M., discussing the message of the gospel presented in the show. Our schedule during these trips is grueling, but these reports inspire us to heed the words of Ephesians 5:15–16, "Be careful how you live, not as unwise but as wise, making the most of every opportunity. . . ." The fascination for our message—a fascination that so inflamed their hearts it kept them from sleep—rendered our small sacrifices of comfort, ease, and sleep pale by comparison.

Four little girls captured our attention in the Gagarian camp. Each day they rushed in to get a seat on the front row, had their Bibles open, and were ready to answer any questions asked. We were impressed to see that their mothers also attended the lessons and the performances. Mary, Tanya's mother and a graduate professor of English at the U.S.S.R. Academy of Sciences in Moscow, approached me after one of the lessons and asked if I might write out the prayer I had prayed for them—a request inspired by her Orthodox background. The Russian Orthodox Church only recited prescribed prayers. If the people wanted to pray, they read one of these prayers. They were not taught to speak directly with God. I explained to Mary that she did not need a written prayer, that she simply needed to talk with God heart to heart.

She invited the team to their cottage to see a skit and listen to some songs that the girls had prepared in English. We had a wonderful time of fellowship with these new Christians from Moscow. And it began a relationship that would have far-reaching consequences for the lives of Mary and Tanya and the future of New Life Ministries.

During our time in Jurmala teaching in the camps, these mothers and daughters were our fan club, walking to other camps to see us perform. We were forming deep friendships, and it was wonderful to see the Holy Spirit unite our hearts. Mary shared how the lessons had dramatically changed their lives. "I can't tell you how you have changed Tanya's and my life. It is incredible. The other night about 4:00 A.M., there was a crazy man outside on the street. The next morning the children were talking about it, and two of them said, 'Let's pray that God would not let him touch us.' But Tanya told them, 'I'm going to pray that he is cured.'"

She related how Tanya prayed every night for a long time. "I can't get her to stop, but I know it is good, so I let her pray." Another parent said that every day the children hurried home to study and prepare for the next lesson. "They never do that in school."

In our conversations with Mary, she provided some valuable insight into the children of the Soviet Union that confirmed what we had discovered in our research. "You see, the children here have not been allowed to be themselves. They must suppress their feelings. They must be like everyone else. You have cared for our children. You have changed our lives. You treat each child as a treasure, as if they are the only ones in the world. It is sure to open their hearts." The week after we met those precious families, I walked down to the cottage from a nearby camp and asked if we might have church with them on Sunday. This service provided a rare opportunity for me to share on worship, a subject about which they knew little. Mary translated for me. I explained that God called us to worship, which means prostrating ourselves before the Lord. In the presence of the Lord, we get vision and strength.

Sharing with them from the Old Testament, I related God's promise to Moses that in the Holy of Holies He would commune with them. I also shared the principles we learned in Helsinki, such as worship's serving as a weapon in spiritual battle and as a source of strength in time of need. We sang through the first side of a Hosanna "Integrity" tape. The tape was in Russian, and we gave them Russian song sheets. The songs were familiar to us, so we sang along in English.

That time of worship was indeed an incredible experience. Two different worlds were united together under the banner of Jesus Christ. He was our common denominator. The presence of the Holy Spirit was so real in that cottage as our praises rose as incense to His throne. Not wanting a single person to miss this experience, I probed, "Can anyone feel the presence of the Lord in this place?" Unable to control her enthusiasm, Alona, one of the shyer little girls, shot up out of her chair and burst forth with an unmistakable "YES!" Her resolute response was echoed in every heart.

With tears in her eyes, Irena shared that her husband had a very serious illness and was in a coma and not expected to live. Through Mary, she explained, "I knew God could purify us, but I never knew He could give us strength . . . While we were singing I could feel some extra strength, and I know God will help get me through this difficult time."

We stopped immediately and prayed for Irena's husband. As tears rolled down her face, she said, "I didn't know that you could do that—just stop and pray for a need."

After worshiping through the second side of the tape, they asked some additional questions, again sorting through the teachings of the Orthodox church. "Can we only worship on Sunday?" "Do we always have to kneel when we pray?" What a tremendous time of discipleship!

Little did we know that this service was preparing Mary's boyfriend, Dima Kanzansky, for a task of immense proportion. He was visiting Mary and Tanya for a few days and attended a performance of *Never Be the Same*. At the invitation, he responded. The following week, he and I had the opportunity to talk at length after a worship service about spiritual warfare. He asked questions about light and darkness, and I detailed the principles of salvation and guidance. Upon his return to Moscow, Dima had to draw on those principles during the August coup attempt to overthrow Gorbachev. God was so gracious in preparing Dima's heart for those trials through the time we shared together.

That time of worship, study, and prayer was a milestone in the lives of those people. A whole new dimension of God's character was revealed to them through that modest, yet powerful, service. Later Mary wrote,

> We all are very thankful to you all for all you have done for us and for all the children of our country. Jesus came to our hearts and I believe He will stay with us forever. I shall pray that we could meet again and that I could help you to serve Jesus. You taught us what it is to have Jesus in our hearts, you taught us how to praise Him and how to serve Him. I can read nothing else now but the Bible. I have to reread some passages over and over again hoping to get closer to the Lord. I can say the same about Tanya. She reads the Bible very slowly and reads it several times a day. I cannot stop thinking about our children in the camps and sanatoriums. How they love you! What great things you are doing for them. How could it be that it was closed for us for such a long time. Yours in Christ, Mary.

Natasha Changa, a young teen-ager we met during the August 1990 tour, was a counselor at the Gagarian camp. What a blessing to see her again. Her English had improved tremendously, enabling us to have some meaningful conversations about her Christian walk. Each day some team members would talk with her about all she learned. One day she asked Sonia about giving thanks before a meal, something she had witnessed the team doing. She queried, "Thanking God is something I have not done, and I realized that I have a lot to be thankful for, so I must thank Him, yes?" Her question certainly impressed upon us the importance of steadfastly living our Christian faith even in small ways like giving thanks before a meal. After a brief discussion, Natasha concluded that saying a prayer before each meal would be a good way for the children to learn to be more thankful, another example of their willingness to apply what they learn.

The building of relationships is what made this trip so rich. God blessed the brief encounters during past trips, but these discipleship sessions allowed us time to nurture friendships of the past and forge new friendships of depth and strength. Driving into Bulduri Sanatorium for a lesson one morning, we were indeed struck with the significance of relationships and our role as Jesus' hands and feet. As we approached the sanatorium, we were listening to a Bob Fitts Maranatha tape. The chorus repeated, "Oh Lord, I receive your love." As the bus slowly backed into the camp, Scott shouted, "Open your eyes and receive God's love." Our eyes fell upon hundreds of smiling and screaming little ones, running from every direction. Across the campus, down the street, through the grass, down hills, children came from everywhere and clamored around the bus. As we watched them dart from every corner of the camp, the chorus continued, "Lord, I receive Your love." Through the adoration of these children, God was reaching down from heaven, reassuring us of His presence and abundant love.

Stepping into what Suzie dubbed "The Backyard of Heaven," the children mobbed us, grabbing our hands and embracing us. Every day, the same scenario transpired. At first sight of the bus, "the Americans are coming" spread through the camp like wildfire, and we were lavished with gleeful cheers and glorious smiles. Moving or even raising our arms was virtually impos-

sible for the children crowding around, hanging onto
our hands. God indeed works through relationships.
Again, we who came to bless received God's blessing in
abundance through the love of these children. Gone
were the days when they demonstrated such caution
around us, afraid to interact. God broke the shackles of
their hearts; and love, once stifled, flowed from them
with ease.

Little Inna studied and listened intently to the lessons. She carried her Bible everywhere in the camp.
We never saw her without it. Inna was timid, but
Sonia made quite a hit with her. At the first glimpse of
Sonia, Inna would run over and grab her hand. The
following is a letter that Sonia received from Inna after
arriving home. It is a perfect example of just how deeply
these children's lives were touched by the team.

> Hallo Sonia! You become my best friend. Thank
> you that you gived me so big present, Bible. No, I
> love Jesus very much. No, I read Bible and pray
> every day. I'll pray for you and for your theater. I
> liked your theater very much. I thank Lord that I
> know you. I love you very much and I'll wait your
> letter every day. Wrait me please. With love Inna.

Exposure is so important with these children, especially with teen-agers. Many children respond to the
message, but the teens are naturally a little more in-
hibited. In many cases, they are counselors and have
an image to maintain with the younger children and
with their peers. Moreover, they have had more time to
nurture the distrust one learns when living under a
Communist regime and in a society corrupted by a
depraved ideology. Befriending these teens shatters
the barriers and allows us to minister to them with no
encumbrances.

Michael, seventeen, a gymnast, and Oleg, twenty-
three, a runner, were two counselors who came to know
Christ because we had the time and took the initiative
to build relationships with them first. Six decisions
were made the day they accepted Christ. Michael and
Oleg walked the aisle with four children. Their deter-

mination and courage to lay hold of Jesus touched our hearts. Discipleship is rich because of resolute decisions like the ones made by these two young men.

This trip provided the added privilege of discipling a group of Armenian children, the majority from Muslim backgrounds. Some of the camps forbid these children entry because they are boisterous and their influence can be disruptive, but the director of Tereskova truly cared for the children and welcomed them. Many of the twelve who attended had lost one or both parents in an earthquake. Naira, a thirteen-year-old from Armenia, had lost both her parents and lived with relatives. When she heard the message of Christ's sacrifice and unconditional love, she responded to the invitation on the first day. This young girl desperately needed the unconditional love of Christ to strengthen her as she learned to accept the cruel death of her parents. Naira overheard the director telling Sonia about her plight. They were speaking in English, but somehow she understood. Overcome anew with grief, she sobbed uncontrollably. Sonia held her and let her cry. How long had those tears been welling inside her? How long had it been since she had a sympathetic shoulder to cry on? Sonia held her and comforted her as she released the pain through her tears. It was no coincidence that Tereskova accepted those children for that August. We knew that through our ministry Jesus reached out to those little ones who harbored such grief. True healing could begin. Sonia taught Naira and some of her friends "Jesus Loves Me" in English. Now whenever these children feel alone and their pain seems unbearable, they will recall that song, hum the tune, and take comfort in Jesus' boundless love.

Leigha, the director of the camp, observed us daily as we ministered to the children. She loved them, but she perceived a difference in our interaction. She commented to Debbie, "They simply adore you; you make each one feel so special." She was curious about how we make each one feel special when we minister to thousands in a year. Leigha had observed us as we spent

hours signing Zack letters, writing a special message
to each child. We truly believe that God could choose to
use that message years later in the lives of these individuals.

Seizing the opportunity, Debbie explained to her
that we treat them special because God lovingly and
carefully created each one. Every child is precious to
our Heavenly Father, and we, as His ambassadors, see
them through His eyes and treat them accordingly.
How wonderful to see God use something as simple as
our interaction with His children to expose the heinous
lie of communism that says individuality is a dirty
word and that humanity means nothing apart from its
utility! The light of His truth was indeed exposing the
darkness.

Inherent in the struggle between light and darkness are Satan's attempts to lure people away from the
truth with spiritual counterfeits. For every God-given
truth, Satan has a seductive counterfeit. Scripture is
clear about his ability to disguise himself as an angel
of light. As the deceit of communism was exposed, the
people began to venture forth in search of something to
fill the void. Tragically, some encountered and are en-
countering the tantalizing spiritual counterfeits of Satan and embracing them as truth. In light of this reality, our work of evangelism and discipleship assumes a
new sense of urgency. Nothing disclosed this truth more
than Debbie and Suzie's conversation with two young
teen-agers.

Marina approached Debbie while they were setting
up for their first show at Tereskova. She had ten years
of English to her credit, so conversation flowed easily.
Marina asked about the show, and Debbie explained
that it was a Christian musical for children. Marina
volunteered that she was a Christian, and Debbie obviously responded with enthusiasm. However, as the
discussion progressed, Debbie began to wonder about
her Christian commitment. She made comments like,
"My grandmother goes to church regularly and occa-
sionally I go with her." Finally, Debbie asked, "Have

you put your trust in Jesus?" She responded, "Yes, I
trust Jesus . . . and me." Now, a little clearer picture.
Like so many of these children, Marina was yet another victim of an ideology that glorified the strength
of man.

Debbie explained that Jesus wants us to trust Him
alone, for we are powerless to earn our salvation. He
was the only One who could pay the penalty for our
sins, and the only means of reconciliation with God
was to put our faith in Him. Debbie also explained that
The Greatest Star of All illuminates these truths. Following the show, there would be an opportunity for her
to pray and ask Jesus to take control of her life. Later,
Debbie and Suzie talked with Marina and her friend,
Vika. Both accepted Jesus as their Savior at the invitation. As they chatted, Vika, via Marina, asked Suzie
her date of birth. The question seemed innocent enough,
yet when Vika received Suzie's reply, she consulted a
notebook. With this notebook, she was going to tell
Suzie her destiny. These two girls were introduced to
the occult through several psychics who were gaining
prominence in the Soviet Union for their teaching and
powers. Astrology and the use of horoscopes in predict-
ing a person's destiny were included in their teachings.

Stopping Vika mid-sentence, Suzie inquired as to
where they received the formula used to foretell one's
destiny. Vika replied, "From a horoscope in a Russian
newspaper." Satan was getting publicity. Silently en-
listing God's guidance, Suzie and Debbie chose their
words carefully, explaining to the girls that God alone
determines our destinies. Marina listened intently and
translated key phrases for Vika as they imparted the
truth that Jesus and these teachings have no common
ground. They explained that Satan would like nothing
better than to distract us from God with his counterfeits, but we must be careful not to fill our minds with
falsehoods. Marina said that she understood the importance of not trying to mix her Christian faith with
these false teachings.

As we walked outside, she shared an insightful perception of the peoples' inner struggle. "You know, we in the Soviet Union have been deprived of religion for so long. Now, as people are realizing the lies of communism, they are looking for something to believe in."

Sue also had a teen-ager approach her after one of the shows and ask if transcendental meditation would interfere in her relationship with Jesus. Gently, Sue questioned her: "What do you do when you meditate?"

"I focus on words I am given," Maya replied.

"Could you focus on Scripture instead?" Sue queried.

"Oh, no! They say you can only use words they give you."

Sue carefully explained that this practice would definitely interfere with her walk with Jesus.

"How could this be? When I meditate I am only clearing my mind, purifying myself." They talked for about fifteen or twenty minutes as Sue related how anything that distracts her from God is not good. She encouraged Maya to read her Bible and ask Him to show her who He is.

"You can ask the Lord to help you see truth and know when others are not telling you the truth about Jesus," Sue said. Inquiring of God was new to this young teen-ager, but she left promising to read her Bible and search for God's truth. Without Christ, these people are easy prey for the evil schemes of Satan. We must hasten to fill the void with truth. Jesus speaks of this need and urgency in Matthew 12:43-45. An unclean spirit "goes out of a man," yet if nothing fills the void, the unclean spirit will return and take along with it "seven other spirits more wicked than itself, and they go in and live there; and the last state of that man becomes worse than the first."

What an ominous, sober warning! Now that the demon of communism has seemingly been exorcised, will we faithfully and urgently bring them truth to fill the void? We do not have to turn back the pages of history very far to find a great parallel with a sobering lesson. It points out the church's unwillingness to seize one of the greatest opportunities for ministry in this century, or perhaps one of the greatest of all time.

After Japan surrendered at the end of World War II, a spiritual vacuum existed in a country that believed its emperor to be god. The resounding defeat at the hands of the allies exposed his fallibility, and he stood before his citizenry an "emperor with no clothes." General Douglas MacArthur recognized the urgency of this moment in history and called on the churches to send as many missionaries as possible to Japan. Only a few responded. Today, Japan is one of the most godless, materialistic nations on earth. Missionaries will tell you how difficult it is to reach the Japanese people.

Tragically, the greatest opportunity of this century— until now—was missed. Eastern Europe and the Commonwealth are ripe for harvest, "but the workers are few" (Matthew 9:37). Over 300 million people throughout this region of the world are hungry for God, as the cults and psychic healers rush in along with Western materialism, pornography, criminal activity, and greed. Will the evil return seven times stronger than before? Only you and I hold the answer as we choose to respond to God's call to "go and make disciples of all nations." These are once-in-a-lifetime open doors.

10

Woe to those who make unjust laws, to those who issue oppressive decrees, to deprive the poor of their rights and withhold justice from the oppressed of my people.

(Isa. 10:1-2)

Military Coup D'Etat

On 19 August 1991, the team was sitting in the Pioneer camp of Kaija when Scott made the following announcement, "There has been a military coup d'état in the Soviet government, and Gorbachev is no longer in power."

They sat motionless, in shock. It was as if the sound of prison doors slamming shut echoed in their ears. Countless questions raced through their minds. What would the future hold for the people of this nation? Would these precious children ever truly experience freedom from the iron fist of communism? Was our work in the Soviet Union finished? Would this camp once again become an organ of the party?

Life at Kaija seemed sheltered from the implications of the political upheaval. The children's smiles and laughter during the next performance belied the seriousness of the day's events, but the team performed with the knowledge that it might be their last opportunity to share the gospel on Latvian soil. For all they knew, the door of freedom had been closed shut just as quickly as it had opened. Why had we not done more while we could?

After the performance, they spotted Mary and Tanya, their expressions weary from fear. Residents of Moscow, they were naturally concerned about the turmoil. Mary was frightened for Dima who had already returned home. Communication was impossible, but

she knew with certainty that he would defend the freedom that opened his way to Christ. In the midst of her
fear, Mary's new faith shone through. "They can take
away many things and scare us, but they can never
take away us praying to God, can they?" As she spoke
these words, Scott wrote later that he could see a "peace
that surpasses all understanding" flood her soul. They
could rob her of many things, but they could never rob
her of her relationship with the Heavenly Father. She
could never be snatched from His hand.

The bus ride into Riga confirmed the team's fears.
Tanks rolled in the streets as did armored personnel
carriers sporting soldiers with machine guns. A little
shaken but cleaving to Christ, the team gathered together in the hotel for prayer and worship. They reviewed the notes from our discussion on David and
Goliath. The truths of this account brought much comfort in a grave time of uncertainty. The teaching that
David, in the midst of adversity, did what he knew to
do, gave them vision for the days ahead. They were
also inspired anew to keep their eyes on Christ in the
knowledge that He was far greater than the "Soviet
military Goliath."

Later that night, Scott wrote these words in his
journal as he kept one eye on the street adjacent to his
first floor window:

> It's 12:30 A.M. The tanks roll through the streets
> every once in a while. We hear that some have been
> shot at the train station. The borders are closed.
> We hear that Moscow's in mayhem—that Yeltsin
> has ordered a general strike—that Latvian officials
> have been seized. The team is frightened at times.
> Rest will be good. We worshipped to side two of
> 'Eternal God' on the way back from Jurmala to-
> night. It was very good. As we returned to Riga, we
> learned there was reason for concern: Tanks on the
> bridge and at the borders, etc. This is real. It is
> happening and God has us here. It's God's timing
> that we're done with Jurmala. Tomorrow we're
> supposed to be at two children's hospitals. My great-
> est hope is to perform.

Latvian television and radio were seized, as well as the phone lines. Communication was impossible. Local television stations here in the States seized the news and began reporting updates on the team's whereabouts. Nationally, USA Radio News broadcast two reports, CBN reported on the team's plight, and three reports aired on James Dobson's "Family News in Focus," which is carried by Christian radio stations across the country. God used a bad situation to focus attention on our mission to reach this desperate land.

The team performed at the two hospitals. Can you imagine the war in the heavenlies? As tanks took their positions in the streets to defend an ideology conceived by Satan, our team performed *The Greatest Star of All*, sharing the gospel and leading hundreds to Christ. They gave out 1,200 Bibles that day alone.

Ironically, the command center of the military operation for the whole Baltic region—Latvia, Estonia, Lithuania—was in a building directly across the street from the hotel. The presence of tanks and soldiers was particularly acute beneath the team's windows. Another vivid illustration of intense spiritual warfare! The team waged battle in prayer and worship in their hotel rooms while military leaders articulated physical strategy only twenty feet away.

Early that morning, at about 3:00 A.M., they began the long trip home at the advice of our host, Sergei Shendrick. Their safety was precarious as long as they stayed in that hotel. Soldiers had commandeered other key buildings. Rumor had it that this hotel was next. Without the use of the phone lines, they could not call ahead to arrange a flight from Tallinn or to determine whether the roads were clear for travel, but Sergei felt they should chance it in light of the strong possibility that the hotel would be seized.

As the team traveled, Dima labored through the night in Moscow, defending the Russian White House. The first night of the coup, an announcement was made via the underground democratic radio that all honest, decent people of Russia who wanted to defend the free-

dom of the country should come to the White House
and stand as part of the human barricades. All official
communication lines were cut, but somehow they managed to broadcast this message without giving away
their location.

Tens of thousands risked their lives venturing into
the streets overrun with tanks and soldiers. They rushed
to the White House where Yeltsin was quartered and
began building barricades in the square. Anything they
could carry from the streets became part of the barriers—logs, parts of cars, cement blocks, tires, building
materials from construction sites in the area. These
barricades were no match for tanks, but they served as
a political statement in opposition to the coup. Never
before had Russian citizens organized against the official government. The democratic deputies, or members
of the legislature, organized five-hour shifts. Those officially listed were not allowed to step aside even for a
minute.

Dima was not listed on the first night but went to
the square several times during the day. On the evening
of 20 August, he took his place on the official list. That
night, there were reports of an attack. As Dima left his
flat to journey to the square, he was uncertain of the
fate that awaited him. He was scared. No one could
predict the events of the evening. If caught, he could be
shot, or at the very least, imprisoned. If the Iron Curtain had slammed shut again, we probably never would
have heard of our friends again.

As he walked and pondered the possible consequences of his actions, a song came to mind. At first, he
could not place it, but then he remembered. It was the
song, "Give Thanks," that he learned at the worship
service with the team in Jurmala. He could not recall
the tune, but he began to repeat the words while the
principles taught during the service echoed in his mind.
Suddenly, he heard the song so vividly that he looked
about for a tape recorder. Could someone be playing it?
He scanned the street. He was alone. Then Dima understood. The song was playing in his head. The Holy

Spirit brought the song to mind when he needed it most. God was reminding him of His help. Over and over again, he heard the words of the chorus, "And now, let the weak say I am strong, let the poor say I am rich, because of what the Lord has done for us."

Fright turned to strength as Dima recognized that he need not feel alone. God walked with him to the square and would stand with him in the barricade. But the assurance was for more than him alone. A certainty that democracy would prevail flooded his being. No attack would be successful. As he stood in the ranks and listened to the speeches delivered by the democratic leaders, he perceived a different atmosphere. The people were uniting in pursuit of a common goal. Division and strife had become a way of life for the Russian people. But that night, a spirit of unity and cooperation predominated. No one could have predicted the events that unfolded. People brought food to the square and shared it with others. Cafes and restaurants contributed to the cause. Even McDonald's brought hamburgers.

Strangers, men and women alike, built fires and stood in groups, listening to the radio and discussing the events. Peril loomed, but the harmony inspired by the evening's events could not escape Dima's notice. The people seemed freed from the self-centered shells that prevented them from caring or reaching out to others. This was so uncharacteristic of these people. It was as if new wineskins were ready for new wine.

There is liberty in fighting for freedom after years of submission. They were in pursuit of a great cause, and they knew it. Dima stood in the barricades, praising God for His unmistakable presence.

About 9:00 P.M., the situation became critical. An icy chill filled the air. The leaders of the coup announced a curfew in hopes of clearing the square. Violation of curfew was a serious offense in the Soviet Union and could bring the harshest penalty—death. Forty minutes later, Yeltsin voided the curfew. He appealed to the masses not to leave the square or the

White House would be seized. The people heeded his
petition and stood their ground. The subways were
packed as streams of people still made their way to the
square. Human barricades formed not only outside the
White House, but also up the street and outside the
American Embassy.

All the leaders of the country, government officials
and prominent professionals, delivered speeches continually, appealing to the consciences of the people and
the soldiers in the square. Men approached the tanks
that squared off against them. "We are Russian, you
are Russian. How can you fire upon us?" Some responded, "No, we promise we will never shoot." Could
their promises hold true? The people knew that disobedience in the ranks incurred the wrath of the regime.

The underground radio broadcast that an attack
was imminent. Tensions escalated. Gas masks were
distributed. No one could tell friend from foe. There
were some military detachments on the side of the
government, but the confusion made it impossible to
ascertain sides.

At 11:00 P.M., the women were told to leave the
square. Paratroopers were expected. It was announced
that in the coming half hour, the entire struggle could
be decided. Soldiers arrived displaying thousands of
pairs of handcuffs. Shots rang out in the distance. They
came from the direction of the American Embassy.

When Dima arrived, blood stained the streets. Some
in the crowd related the events. A tank had turned
toward the crowd, poised to attack. One man attempted
to stop it by blocking the driver's vision with a blanket.
The soldiers pulled him through the hatch in the tur-
ret, shot him, and hung his body on the outside as an
example to all. When a second man attempted to remove the body, the tank ran him down. Then it stopped.
A soldier ran from it. Another man tried to stop him,
and he was shot.

The other Republics saw no bloodshed. Tanks were
positioned in all the capital cities, but there was little
movement. Communication was severed from Russia,

so no one could follow the struggle. But they knew that their destiny would be decided in Moscow. Everyone waited.

The night of 20 August decided the fate of the coup and the country. The leaders of the KGB and the military did not expect opposition from the people. The masses always succumbed in the past to any show of force. That night they acted in strength. It frightened the leaders of the coup that even in the face of bloodshed the people did not yield. Confusion in the ranks caused by the organized and united opposition finally convinced the military leaders that the coup would never succeed. It officially aborted the insurrection the following day.

The three courageous victims of this insurgency were symbolic of the unity inspired by the day's events. The first gentleman fought in the Afghanistan invasion. Afghanistan was Russia's Vietnam. Consequently, these soldiers were treated badly upon their return. But they were always among the first to fight for justice.

The second was a Jewish architectural student. Anti-Semitism predominates in Russia. Many are forced to emigrate to the United States or to Israel, wreaking havoc on many Jewish families.

The third victim was the oldest. He was an employee of a joint venture, or cooperative business agreement, between Russia and another country. In other words, he was a benefactor of Russia's new freedoms—a newborn businessman.

Millions attended the funeral honoring those men. They paid their last respects to three individuals with diverse backgrounds and priorities who united in a desperate quest to defend freedom. People carried banners, and the streets were decorated with their pictures. They met at the Kremlin and then at the White House. Millions of people participated in the procession—again uniting with common purpose and celebrating the victory for which these men fought.

I think back to a quieter, more peaceful day, when Dima and I talked while standing in the ocean breeze of Jurmala. Who could have imagined then how we would touch history? Never underestimate the impact of the seed of God sown in a heart. A pebble lying on the shore holds no force. But tossed into a pond, it ripples the water as waves move out from its point of impact. Recently, a sermon I heard summed it all up. The speaker, a pastor from Fayetteville, North Carolina, aptly entitled the message, "History belongs to those who pray." May we live by those words.

11

If my people, who are called by my name, will humble themselves and pray and seek my face and turn from their wicked ways, then will I hear from heaven and will forgive their sin and will heal their land.

(2 Chron. 7:14)

Glimpses of a Nation Transformed

Following every tour, we write to the children of the Commonwealth, encouraging them in their new relationship with Christ and prompting them to read and study their Bibles. Consequently, we receive many beautiful letters from children and parents expressing their gratitude and sharing the joy that Christ brought to their lives. This chapter will share some of those heartwarming letters as well as some written prayers that were prompted by our correspondence. Envision a nation transformed as you read of their new love for Christ and their desire to learn all about Him. Rejoice with us as they ask questions demonstrating their genuine desire to learn and grow in their newfound faith. Not every letter will awe you with its depth, but remember even the simplest expressions of faith, love, and friendship are glimpses of new life.

* * * * *

Hello!

I was very glad to get your letter. Thank you very much! I liked your musical very much and I am looking forward to your coming. I want to tell you that I'll try to "grow" in my new life. I took Jesus Christ into my heart and I am giving my life into His hands.

I've read several times the children's Bible and some other Christian literature. I liked some quotations from

the Bible and I memorized some of them. For example
this one: "For God so loved the world that He gave His
only begotten Son that whosoever believed in Him would
not perish but have everlasting life."

Thank you very much!
Ann

* * * * *

Hello, my friend Gulley!
Write to me everything about Jesus and God. I
want to know all about them. I want to live according
to Jesus' words and become a member of His family.
Mr. Gulley, I'll wait for your letter and for a new lesson. I hope you'll write to me. Good-bye.

Your friend,
Julia

* * * * *

Hello!
Do you remember your performance in the Gagarin
pioneer camp? I asked you to give me your address. I
was amazed by your performance and I decided to ask
for your address so that you could write me and I could
write you. I have only one wish—to know more about
our Lord, Jesus Christ. Please write to me about Him.
I know that He was born in Bethlehem and that He
had 12 disciples and that one of them—Judas—betrayed
Jesus and only 11 disciples were left. But after Jesus
was crucified one more disciple came to Him and so
there became 12 of them again. But I want to know
more about Him.

* * * * *

Greg,
You said that I can share my troubles and joys with
you. Please tell me what to do. A boy loves me, but I
hate him because I love another boy, Oleg. The one
whom I hate is called Grisha. Please advise me what to
do. I've tried to discuss it with my mother, but she
doesn't want to hear. I ask you very much.

Natasha

* * * * *

Hello Zack,

Let Jesus bring peace and joy to you.

Everything is okay with me. I study at school, I play with dolls though I am already 9. On Sundays, I with my Daddy go to the church and to Sunday school, where I together with other children study the Bible. . . .

Let love and joy fill your heart on the day when our Lord was born and let love and joy stay in your heart all new 1992.

Tanya Bragina

* * * * *

Dear Greg,

I congratulate you from the bottom of my heart with the coming 1992 year. Let every day and every hour be happy for you. . . . Write me! Please write more often. I grow in Jesus everyday!

Julia

* * * * *

My Dear Friends,

I am well. How are you? I want to see you. Now, I live with Christ. I read my Bible. I like to read Bible very much.

Your Eoel

* * * * *

Hello Zack, teacher of wild animals!

I am your friend, Dmitry Sirotko. I have read the book New Testament. I've liked it very much. It is very interesting. I've learned a lot of new things about Jesus. I am going to read it for the second time. . . . Things are not bad at school. I have good and excellent marks in school. But things are not so good with money and housing. Father wants to get some private farm but he has not enough money. . . . But we live not as bad as others. I know that Jesus will help them and me. I believe in Jesus.

Dmitry

* * * * *

Hello my dear friend!

I am Victor—your new friend who is eager to be saved as any person who has sinned on this sinful planet. I am so glad and very thankful to you for your attention to me. Also, I am very grateful to you for "good news" which I have got from you. I together with my family (my wife Vera and my son Oleg) are lonely in this small town and we are waiting to be saved. But we cannot get it any time because the enemy of our souls tries to put as many obstacles as he can, tries to tempt our souls, but we hope only for our Star—Jesus Christ.

To communicate with other people (with believers) we must go very far to other towns and we cannot always do this. And in our town, there are no true Christians and without communication it is difficult to keep the temperature [temperament?] which we need so much to be saved. That is why, dear Zack, we ask you and our relatives in Christ to pray for us, feeble ones. And we will be thankful to our Jesus for you.

Dear friend, if you have the possibility to send us tapes with Christian recordings—songs, stories—will you kindly send us and we in our turn will be very thankful to you and your friends?

Best wishes to Leopard, Tiger, Bear and Clowns.

Your friend,
Victor

* * * * *

Thank you for the interesting letter and present—book Jesus Christ. You are very kind.

I am 10 years old. I am school boy. I love God.

I like to go to the school on Sunday where study Bible. I should very much like do you present.

God Bless you!
Sergei

* * * * *

Dear Friends!

I love to congratulate you.

Marry Christmass. I glad to share our holiday with my American brothers and sisters. This holiday became a great event for me. I wish you all of love, care, happy feelings that all God could give.

Your Brother In Christ,
Andrew

* * * * *

Greg!

I congratulate you with New Year and Christmas! God bless you and all your family. God loves you and we carry Him in our hearts.

Nadeschda

* * * * *

Hello Zack, Leopard, Tiger, Bear, and Clowns,

That's me, Ilona Stupak whom you've sent the Bible "New Testament." Thank you once again for having sent it to me. . . . I live well and I learn more and more about Jesus and His miracles from the Bible. I read about the deeds of His disciples and write down some answers in my notebook. . . .

In the morning and in the evening, I pray speaking with God. But sometimes I do not know what to tell him. Please teach me, give me advice. What can I speak about?

Please write me.

Ilona Stupak

* * * * *

Hello Brandon!

I am Sasha. Do you remember, we met in summer in Jurmala in the camp named after Jan Rainis. You showed a play about Jesus Christ. I have read several times already the book which you have given to me Life of Jesus Christ. . . . Please send me two Bibles if you can do it. One for me, the other for my granny. They cost 80-105 rubles each in our country and we cannot buy them. So if you can please send them.

Brandon, I have one question for you. Why did earlier Jesus come to me in my dreams and now not?

Sasha

* * * * *

Hello Zack, my new friend!

My name is Alexei. I am 19. I study at Riga Technical University. I live in the centre of Riga.

Thank you very much for your letter and for the Bible. Now I have the possibility to learn the Bible and to grow in Jesus Christ. My friends and I have a dream to organize our own Christian club for Bible studies, watching video films about Jesus Christ, communicating with friends, speaking about Jesus. But unfortunately we do not have enough money for it. I hope our dream will come true.

Zack, if you have any possibility of come, please come. I will be very glad to invite you. Please answer me. I shall be waiting for your letter.

I wish you all the best. God bless you!

Sincerely yours,
Alexei

* * * * *

Dear Zack!

I am very touched by your attention and by the present you have sent to me. The present is very dear to me and it touched my heart so much, as the religion which I profess is an Orthodox one and their religion means alot in my life. And due to the Bible which you've sent I'll manage to communicate with God closer and more. And as I am going to be a teacher in the future, I think that it is necessary as only due to the religion and communication with God and Jesus a man can become kinder and purer and to give a part of himself to people.

Again, thank you for your kindness and kindheartedness.

Faithfully yours,
Kata

* * * * *

Hello, my new friends: Zack, Leopard, Tiger, Bear and Clowns!

Hello from a far-away Republic of Latvia. I was very glad to get your letter and I'm also glad to answer it.

We liked your performance called "The Greatest Star of All" very much. I saw it with my son and my mother. . . . On the day of our meeting after the performance I with my son went forward. He touched the tail of Leopard with interest and then gave Leopard a hug. Dear Leopard, do you remember it? You said, What a beautiful child!

Yes, my sonny whose name is Andrew is really handsome. . . . But in a man everything must be beautiful—not only his looks but his soul as well. I'll try to bring my children up so that they would love Jesus and others.

Jesus comes to every person who asks Him to come and makes a new man out of him. Lately, I've tried to act as Jesus wants me to. I do not seem to feel anything special but my life is changing and of course for the best.

I love Jesus and I hope that I am loved by Him and that is why I am very happy.

God bless you for good deeds and intentions.

Sincerely yours,
Angella Markevich

* * * * *

Hello Zacharias, Leopard, Tiger, Bear and Clowns!

I am your friend Ilona whom you have sent the Bible. Thank you very much for it. I like it very much because it tells about the life of Jesus Christ. Earlier I do not believe that God existed. But in the sanatorium there was a girl who believed in God. She told us that it was better to believe in God than to turn our backs on Him. . . . Your performances in the sanatoriums and the words of my friend made a path in my heart to Jesus. He loves us very much and He will never leave us if we follow His 10 commandments. Thank you for helping us to believe in Jesus. . . .

Good-bye!

Ilona

* * * * *

Hello my dear friend Zacharias,

Ann from the USSR is writing to you. I have got your parcel. Thank you very much for it. My parents were also very glad. My granny was the one who liked it especially she has told me a lot about Jesus. I've already read the book "The Life of Jesus Christ." I liked it very much. And there was so much kindness, unconditional love, and generosity in your performances that I was glad that I would see them.

I try to pray every day. In our country, people are beginning to return to Jesus, to go to churches. . . .

Best wishes to everybody!

Love,

Ann

* * * * *

How do you do Greg!

Well, I'll tell you a few words about myself. I have lived in the city of Norilsk since 1984 together with my family. I've got father, mother, and a younger brother. . . . Recently, they have begun to build a new church in our city. I have also given some money to it. You know, Greg, probably Jesus has really come to my heart. It often seems to me lately that somebody takes control of what I do. Sometimes I see dreams that frighten me. Write to me, Greg, if this is normal. Or is that just my imagination?

Write to me my friend.

Oleg

* * * * *

Dear Greg Gulley!

Thank you very much for the letter. I thank the Lord and you brothers and sisters for praying for us. I go to a Sunday school of a Lutheran church and we also pray for all the people in the world. . . . The Bible is read to me by my parents and teachers of the Sunday school.

* * * * *

Dear Jesus,

I address you from the depth of my heart. I want to follow your words, I want to obey only you and fulfill everything what you told people who you lived on the earth. You take me and send your Holy Spirit so that I could everyday follow you so that I could do everything you want us to do. Help me, Jesus, to grow in you. Do not turn your face from me. Forgive me all my sins. Bless me in what I do. Glory to you, my Lord. Amen.

* * * * *

Hello, Dear Greg Gulley!

I and my wife are very thankful for the letter you've sent our son. He is only eight. And for the first time in his life he got a letter addressed personally to him. There was no end to his surprise and joy. And I and my wife were very glad that this first letter came with the words of Jesus Christ. Truly, Gospel is good news.

Once again let me thank you for the thing you are doing. Let God help you and all your friends.

> Sincerely yours,
> Roman Zelentsov and his
> father Boris Zelentsov

* * * * *

Hello Dear Zack!

My name is Irena. I am from Riga. I'm 14. I am in the 8th grade.

I'd like to learn more about Jesus and God. I love them very much and I'd like to learn more about them.

Could you send me something from what I could learn more about Jesus and God. I choose the way of love and obedience to God, the way of life and kindness.

> Sincerely yours,
> Irena

* * * * *

Lord!

I love you. I am giving you my life. Bless me for good deeds.

* * * * *

Hello!

My name is Julia. I've lost any hope to get your letter and then I got your letter for which I am very grateful. My friends Sveta and Dasha have also got the letters. I do not know about them but I decided to answer your letter. I learned about Jesus and about God not only from your letter. Two girls came to my house. There were 14-15 years old.

A man came with them. He turned out to be an American. I was so embarrassed that I do not even remember his name. We were talking about God. They asked different questions and told us about Jesus. They gave me a New Testament and on that day, I asked Jesus to come into my heart.

I can say that my life has changed since that day. It has changed for the best. I have somebody to share good and bad news with. I pray everyday before going to bed, but I do not use memorized prayers. I pray in my own words. And you know He helps me in everything. . . .

I want to ask you: which Bible should I read? A children's or adults' Bible? And one more question: What is the difference between the Orthodox belief and the Catholic one? I know some people who pray to an icon. Are these people wrong?

I am waiting for your answers and for your letter.

Julia

* * * * *

Hello my new dear friends!

My name is Natasha. I am 16. I live in Kiev.

In summer 1991, I was in Jurmala in the pioneer camp and I'll never forget your wonderful preaching. I've never before seen anything like this. What you are doing is wonderful. We were amazed where you get so much energy, love for life. It seems to us that your work is very difficult but very interesting and useful. I personally have learned a lot about the life of Jesus Christ and the history of the first church.

The book given by you—the book about Jesus—became one of my favorite books. Thank you very much. You are very kind and good people. I love you very much and want to see you. I believe that Jesus Christ is alive.

Your new friend,
Natasha

* * * * *

Dear Friends!
Thank you for your letter. I am very grateful to you for the book.

I have read your book. I not all understand, but I try comprehend meaning of reading.

I have a question I should like to ask you. Many people read this book, but much people do sin. Why? Do me a favor. Write me an answer.

Your friend,
Oleg

* * * * *

Hello Greg!
My name is Nadeja. I got a letter from you long ago and I'm sorry that I couldn't answer for such a long time. . . .

Greg, I'd like to know why Jesus called to help people doesn't give common sense to those who are creating so much evil? People who steal, bureaucrats and even murderers are leading such a good life now, they are multiplying and are afraid of nobody. Why are there so many poor, sick, unhappy people? I am very sorry for those who live in Petersburg. They became absolutely different people—hard, cruel, angry, and their souls are dirty.

Now it is not time to pay somebody back. We must

help each other, pray for each other so that peace and kindness could come to our land. Every day before going to bed, I read the Bible trying to memorize it and pray for those who are far away from me, whom I think of and love very much.

I want ignorance and evil to go away, as well as lie and deceiving. People must stop killing each other.

Thank you for your prayers for me. I am praying for you.

Nadeja

* * * * *

O, my Lord, my Savior, make me chosen a right way in my life and let me and my family be happy. Amen.

Jimur

* * * * *

Dear Zack!

I liked your performance very much. I liked the actors though I saw the performance for the second time. I believe in God, but I know only one prayer that you told us in Riga at school N30. I memorized it, but I want to know more prayers and be able to pray. I have only one prayer: Dear Lord Jesus Christ! I love you. Thank you for dying for me on the cross. Please forgive my sins. Come into my heart, Lord Jesus, and help me to live for you all my life. I love you Jesus Christ. Amen.

* * * * *

Hello Dear Zack and Greg! With great joy I got and read your letter. Thank you very much for it! I will follow your advice. I pray every day trying not to miss a single minute. When I have free time I speak with God and Jesus Christ for Jesus will help me to live through unhappy moments and happy ones, will give me advice what to do. A teenager has so many problems but there are few people who understand it. Belief in Jesus will help us to find the right way.

Good-bye. See you soon! Thank you for everything.

Your Anna

* * * * *

Dear Greg Gulley!

My name is Oksana.

When I got your letter I became very happy. I opened it immediately and read it. But while reading it I had some questions.

Where did God come from? What was the first thing that God created on the earth? What are angels? Where did they come from? Who is their father and mother?

If you can, write about yourself. And send me your picture.

Good-bye. Please try to do what I've asked you and please answer my questions.

Your Oksana

* * * * *

Hello, Greg Gulley!

Thank you for the letter you've sent me.

I am interested in one question. What day should be a holiday: Saturday or Sunday? I ask you very much to answer.

I'd like very much to have some Christian fiction and if possible one or two tapes with your musicals.

I am sorry that I ask you so much but I want to come closer to the Lord, to give Him all my life. I am writing about my wishes from the depth of my heart. Because life with God is a right way, I am absolutely sure in it. A great struggle is going on in my heart everyday.

I am waiting for your letter. God Bless you.

Your Lia

* * * * *

Dear Greg!

I know so little about you. But I am sure that those who go preaching Gospel to other people will never fail. God bless you!

Inna

* * * * *

God, my Lord, protect me from an evil force, so that I should follow only the right way. I pray every day so that you could not doubt my belief. I want you to come into my heart and guide [my] life. I will follow your will in the name of the Father, Son, and the Holy Spirit. Amen.

* * * * *

Blessed be you, Lord! I am giving you my heart. Be my guide and advise me in everything I do. For many years, I have sinned but not always it was because I wanted to. I lived in the society where atheism was the main ideology, even mentioning you was laughed at and refused. My eyes opened only during 2 last years and I ask you to forgive me, Lord, and bless me on good actions and thoughts. I ask you also to bless all my family.

Zita

* * * * *

Jesus!
I come to you the way I am. I believe that you've died for my sins and have been resurrected from the death to give me an eternal life. I thank you for having saved me and brought me to a new life. By my God. Thank you for giving me the possibility to become God's child through belief in you. I confess that Bible is God's Word and now all that it says belongs to me.

Irina

* * * * *

Lord, forgive me for all the sins. And judge me the way you judge all the sinners. For us you had to die on the cross. Forgive me, Lord, for everything and judge me.

Inessa

* * * * *

Oh, Lord, you've suffered for us and I give you the right to guide me in the way you like because you've suffered so much and know what the best way to do things.

Eternal Slaver of the Lord,
Sergei Kazpenko

* * * * *

Dear Lord!
I ask you to forgive all my sins and become my Savior and Lord. I ask you to be in full control of my life and to make me the way you'd like to see me. Amen.

Tanya

* * * * *

These letters, with their many questions and requests for correspondence, demonstrate the importance of follow-up with the children of the Commonwealth. We must continue to feed their hunger for the Word and assist them in developing an intimate relationship with their Savior.

Our ministry is currently working on a strategy that will go beyond the six-session discipleship series in answering the need for more in-depth instruction and encouragement. We are calling it our F.U.T.E. ministry (Follow-up Team). This team will be composed of four to six veterans, all with at least two years experience with our ministry. They will travel overseas for three months at a time, leading two-week discipleship programs in places we have already ministered.

Over a dozen current veteran team members indicated recently a stirring in their hearts toward the vision. The F.U.T.E. strategy and materials were developed and tested with four Latvian youth who spent nine weeks with us as part of what we call "The Great Exchange." Twelve sessions were developed that take these young people deeply into God's Word and into relationship with Him. We envision this ministry having an impact not only on children and teen-agers, but also on whole families.

12

Arise, shine; for your light has come, and the glory of the Lord has risen upon you. For behold, darkness will cover the earth, and deep darkness the peoples; but the Lord will rise upon you, and His glory will appear upon you. And nations will come to your light, and kings to the brightness of your rising.

(Isa. 60:1-3)

Three Russians Speak

A Revolution of tremendous proportion grips the Commonwealth—a revolution of the heart. God is reaching out to a nation oppressed for decades, drawing them unto Himself. And they are responding, running to His light. The following is an interview with Mary Adoskina, a graduate professor of English at the U.S.S.R. Academy of Sciences in Moscow who now works with us in our office; her nine-year-old daughter, Tanya; and Dmitry Kanzansky, a Moscow businessman we followed during the August coup. These individuals are just three of the thousands whose lives have been transformed by God's love.

When I think of this talk with Mary, Dima, and Tanya, and Christ's love radiating from their faces, my mind races back to Vadim, the young man certain that God had damned his country to a wretched existence. To Vadim, Christ was the fool's escape. After all, could this Jesus feed him?

The testimonies of Mary, Dima, and Tanya stand in sharp contrast to his bitter perspective. Vadim remains a captive of his miserable circumstances while these three new babes in Christ are experiencing true liberty for the first time in their lives. They opened their hearts to a sustenance that only God provides. In faith, they reached out to the Father, and He rescued them from the impoverished existence that still imprisons Vadim. Your heart will stir as you read of Christ's

transforming power in the lives of these individuals
and their perception of His impact upon the
Commonwealth's people. Mary and Dima offer insight
into existence under an oppressive Soviet regime, the
effect of an evil ideology upon the citizenry, and the
volatile condition of the Republics since the fall of communism. Most important, they explain why Christ is
the Commonwealth's only hope for the future.

Please understand that while New Life Ministries
is mentioned frequently in this interview, it is not my
intention to boast. The purpose of this chapter is to
glorify God, the orchestrator of our endeavors, to demonstrate what He can accomplish through surrendered
hearts, and to communicate the importance of Christ's
light to a nation in the clutches of darkness.

* * * * *

Greg: Mary, share how you met the team and how
the children responded to them.

Mary: In August 1991 I happened to be in Jurmala,
Latvia. I was there on vacation with my daughter, and
I came to a pioneer camp situated across the street
from our cottage. There I met the Red Team giving
their performance, *The Greatest Star of All*.

They did it in the following way: First, they gave
the musical, *The Greatest Star of All*, then four biblical
lessons, and then their second musical, *Never Be the
Same*. I was amazed at seeing the response of the
Soviet children.

I must say that the Soviet children are absolutely
unlike American children. They are very reserved, they
are very shy. It is due to their teachers' trying to kill all
the initiative in them, the teachers' trying to make
them all the same. Their pioneer leaders and the directors of the camps tried to prepare them for meeting the
Americans, but the children did not understand what
was going to happen there.

When the first musical began, I think the children,
at the beginning, were rather reserved, but then as the
musical progressed, I could see, and I was amazed at

seeing it, how their hearts began to open step by step, so to say. In the end of the first musical, all of them, practically everybody who was in the pioneer camp, went forward to the stage and kneeled, praying and asking Jesus to come into their hearts.

They not only loved, they just adored the team members. They waited and waited for them to come to their camp again for a new lesson. They would wait for the bus in which the team members traveled. That was the famous red bus. And the very minute when the children saw the bus all of them would rush into the street, surround the bus, and then they would meet the team members. Every child knew which team member to follow, and they would follow them as little shadows, and they would help them to load and unload the truck, to make-up, to set the decorations on the stage, and they would not leave them in peace for a single minute there.

When the team members had to leave them, they would cry and cry, and they would wave seeing the bus going away. Now they write letters to them saying they are so happy to have Jesus in their hearts, and they are sorry their parents and their friends do not know what they know. Lots of them write, "I love Jesus. Thank you for bringing His love to me, and I love you. I miss you so much. Please come to me, please come to my country again."

Greg: Mary, your nine-year-old daughter, Tanya, also came to know Christ through the ministry of the Red Team. What impact did it have on her life?

Mary: My daughter was among the children who managed to see the musicals and who then prayed, asking Jesus to come into their hearts. She also adored all the team members. She got the Bible. I must say that their team members distributed Bibles, and every child was given a wonderful illustrated Bible in the Russian language. The Bibles are very difficult to get in Russia because there are not many children's Bibles there and they are very, very expensive.

Even at the church, they sell the Bibles. These

Bibles were free, and they were illustrated. It was very
good. It was very helpful for children who have never
heard anything about God, about Jesus.

She got the Bible and she began reading and reading the Bible. She was absorbed in reading the Bible,
and she did not want to stop reading it. She tried to do
her best to be ready for the next biblical lesson. She
was very, very active at these lessons. All of the children at the pioneer camps were very active at the
lessons. This is unusual for them because at schools
the teachers do not like them being as active as they
were at the biblical lessons. It was due to the attitude
of the team members to them. They treated every child
as the dearest child, as a precious stone, if I can say so.
So much kindness, so much love was coming from them
that children could not but feel it and could not but try
to answer, to answer all they could. They tried to take
everything that they were taught in their hearts. They
really did take it all in their hearts.

I mean my daughter, because she was taught, all of
them were taught, the principle GROW. And GROW, if
we decipher it, is Go to Jesus in prayer, Read the Bible
every day, Obey God, and Witness—witness about God.
She remembered all the principles she was taught. The
last principle is witness and, you see, she tried to do
what she was told. So she took everything directly, all
that she was taught. Two weeks later when she came
to Moscow, she had a lesson of home reading at her
school. It was amazing that she tried to share there, to
share there the truth about Jesus. All the children
were asked to bring their favorite books, and she
brought the Bible. She showed the children the Bible,
she tried to tell them all she knew about Jesus, and she
even tried to teach them how to pray. I do not know
how she managed to do this, but I think she did manage to sound convincing because the children seemed
to be very interested in the Bible and in Jesus. You see,
it was miracle, because the children could have made
laugh of her, and the teacher could have made laugh of
her, but not a single one laughed. I think it was due to

God speaking in her at the moment, God helping her to sound convincing. You see, a little child, a new Christian, managed to set little fire on the hearts of her classmates.

Tanya is a true follower of Jesus. Her dream in life is now to be a missionary. She really tries to obey God, and she reads the Bible, and she reads the Bible every day. She is now reading the Bible for the third time. No matter how tired she is, she will read some pages of the Bible before bed. I'm sure that she knows a lot of verses now by heart.

Greg: Share your testimony, about your background, your belief in God before you came to Christ and how you came to Jesus Christ in August.

Mary: As for me, I've always believed in God as a person can believe in kindness and justice, but I have never had any personal relations with Jesus. I just did not know how it could be to have personal relations with Jesus. The Orthodox Church does not teach us how one can speak with Jesus. In the Orthodox Church, we are to learn some prayers by heart. Most of them are in the old Russian language, and personally, I do not understand what they mean, and so it was rather difficult for me to find my way, my direct way, to God. I just could not imagine that I could speak with my own words addressing Jesus. That is why my first question to Greg, that was not only my first question, but the questions of my friends there, was, "Can you give us a certain prayer, so that we could memorize it?"

When we heard them praying, it seemed to us that their prayers were closer to us and they were much more understandable. That is why we asked for a prayer to memorize. It was so amazing for me when he told me that we need not memorize any prayers, that the only thing was to try to think of Jesus as your closest friend and just open your heart to Him, to speak from heart to heart. It turned out to be so easy. I just cannot understand those people who do not want, who think it is difficult to do this. It turned out to be so simple, and I cannot imagine how it can be otherwise.

Jesus responded to my call immediately. He answered all my prayers. I asked Him to try to help me to change my life, and He really did change my life. He changed my life, being in my life, in my heart. And one of His changes is that I am here now working with New Life Ministries trying to bring gospel to my land. That is the only way to heal this country that is in such a terrible situation now.

Greg: Mary, before you came to know Christ, what did the Bible mean to you? What was your exposure to it? And then after you came to the Lord, how did you relate to the Word of God, and what impact did reading the Word and praying have on your life?

Mary: Well, the Bible was something absolutely unknown and new to me. I could not stop reading the Bible. It was like opening a new world for me, but it was not so easy for me to comprehend all the verses. So I had to read and reread the verses again and again, trying to understand their meaning and seeing the truth.

Now, after I was discipled here, I can understand the Bible more and more. More and more things are opening to me, and I am just amazed at reading the Bible, at it opening for me the truth about our life, about the world.

Greg: Share with us your experience during prayer soon after you returned to Moscow.

Mary: My experience was one day it happened maybe two or three weeks after I took Jesus into my heart. Suddenly, I preferred to pray in darkness and alone. Now, I am not sure that I would like to do this. Now, I enjoy praying with other people. But in Moscow, we were the only Christians that we knew there. And so I preferred to pray in darkness.

And one day, it seemed to me that I could feel the hands of God embracing me, and I could really feel myself being in His arms, feeling His strength and His love for me.

Greg: Tell me about your parents, what they do, and what they think about your commitment to Christ.

Mary: My father is an actor. Many people know him in Russia. My mother is a choreographer, a rather famous choreographer in Russia. She danced at the Bolshoi theater and stages at the Bolshoi and other theaters in our country and around the world. Maybe their experience with God is a little more mature than mine because I think that they have known more about Jesus, especially my father. But I think that they tried not to discuss this question when I was a child because it was really very dangerous.

My father's and my mother's grannies were believers, and they could not but influence my parents. My father knows the Bible. He has always known it. He knows it pretty well. They tried to pray, and they tried to ask Jesus to come in their hearts, too, but I wish they could find themselves among Christians here. I think that it would have a great impact on their lives. Now being in Russia, they cannot fully comprehend what it is to be a real Christian.

Greg: Before glasnost and perestroika, you were required to take courses in Marxism-Leninism and atheism. What did they teach you as truth?

Mary: They tried to get us to believe that there is no God, that man can do anything without God's help and that not God, but nature, created the world. They base their ideas on the principles of evolution introduced by Darwin. They tried to give us certain rules according to which all in life develops, that everything has its own reason for having taken place. They tried to convince us that there is no God and there is no faith and only you are responsible for your future, for what you are doing.

Greg: So all the teachers and all those involved in the education of the children had to take these courses?

Mary: Absolutely! All of the teachers, not only all of the teachers, all of the people who get higher education. They must study these courses: Marxism-Leninism, their philosophy, their economy, and atheism.

Greg: Mary, you were our translator when we met
with the Deputy Minister of Culture and the Deputy
Minister of Education of Russia. Share your impressions of those historic meetings.

Mary: That is really miraculous. Though I have
known that religion is officially recognized in the country now, I could not believe that the leaders of the
Ministries could be as sympathetic as they were and
they would try to do all they could to bring your ministry into the country. Both the Deputy Minister of
Culture and Deputy Minister of Education in Russia
said that they would do everything that they could to
help the team members in Russia. They said that all
the theaters, all the schools in Russia, millions of
schools, and thousands of theaters were opened for
them for their noble activity. They would not only not
lay obstacles, but they would try to help. That was
amazing to me because, you see, one could not imagine
earlier that Ministers of Culture and Education could
be as helpful as they were.

Greg: What did the Deputy Minister of Education
say and promise?

Mary: He said that he would fax their directors of
schools in all districts of Russia to make sure that they
would allow New Life Ministries to come to their schools
and to show their musicals. Then he named the number of the schools—64,000 schools in Russia only. He
said that all of them could be ministered to by New
Life Ministries.

Greg: Share some of the letters from children.

Mary: The children, their letters are very charming and moving letters. You can feel so much love
coming from their letters, and so much trust in the
members of New Life because they really write all the
things that are very dear to their hearts. That means
that they consider the New Life members their best
friends.

They answer a lot of questions based on the Bible.
We asked them to answer these questions, and some of
them have already written us letters answering the

questions. Lots of them express their wish that their friends, their mothers and fathers, their brothers and sisters, could know what they know now. Many of them ask to send them the Bibles. They ask, "Please send me sixty Bibles because I want to distribute them among my friends." That means that they are little witnesses, too, now. I wanted to say that they speak a lot about their relations with God in their letters. They ask many questions. They ask advice. They want the team members to give them some advice. Plus, they write the thing that is most dear to them in their hearts. The last letter that I translated was addressed to Greg. That was from a girl who is about fourteen-years-old. She answered all our questions, Bible questions, there. And then there was a little note that followed the letter. She told Greg about her love. And she said that "I am writing it to you, thinking that you are my best friend." And she even couldn't share it with her mother, and with not even a single friend of hers. That means how dear Greg and other people of the ministry are to the Soviet children.

Greg: What do you think would happen in Russia if many people were to come to know Christ as you do?

Mary: I think that only God can change the situation in my country and can heal the land because people in my country, due to the terrible economic and political situation, are very aggressive and cruel now. Only God can break their hearts and bring kindness and love to their lives, even in the present situation. I wish every person could know what I know now about Jesus. I wish every person could have the Bible I have now, because from my own experience, I can feel how great changes can be if you ask Jesus to change your life.

If they become real Christians, I think that first of all, their hearts would melt, their hearts would be very kind. All this terrible bloodshed would stop in my country. Definitely! People would try to serve. If all people in my country were Christians, God would melt their hearts. They would never be as aggressive and cruel as they are now. So all this bloodshed between nationali-

ties would definitely stop in the country. I think that
people would become wiser and try to serve each other,
and they would just try to be all together. And I think
that being together and understanding the truth about
life and about Jesus would help them to survive even
under the present conditions and be wise enough to
wait until the situation is changed. I'm sure that all
their joined actions, joined actions of Christians, could
bring a good life to my land. Definitely that life would
not be a Communist regime.

* * * * *

Greg: Tanya, share with us how you came to know
Jesus.

Tanya: I learned about Jesus from the New Life
Ministries. They give us certain tasks. They asked us
to find verses in the Bible where it was taught about
Jesus. Every time they sang some songs, and we prayed
every time. That happened at the biblical lessons that
they gave in Jurmala.

Greg: How did you feel after you asked Jesus into
your heart? How did your life change?

Tanya: I came to love Him so much. I really felt the
necessity to tell everybody about Him.

Greg: What do you hope New Life can do for the
children of the Commonwealth? Do you think our efforts are important?

Tanya: Yes! Their activity is very important. And
I wish that they could tell our children what I know,
that they could teach them their lessons so that our
children could also learn the truth.

Greg: What do you want to be when you grow up
and why?

Tanya: I want to be one of the members of New
Life. I love God, and I want to be an actress. That is
why I think that my place will be among the members
of New Life.

Greg: What have you learned about the Lord since
you've been in the United States?

Tanya: That you should love Him very much and that He will always help you. He will always help your friends if they are in trouble and if you pray for them. He is sure to help them.

Greg: Tell us about sharing Christ with your friends at school.

Tanya: At school, we have such subject, home reading. We are given such topics, and we are to bring books. And we were asked to bring our favorite books which were read during our summer holidays. I brought the Bible. When I was called by the teacher, I began sharing. Everybody was listening with great attention, and my teacher helped me a little. I explained to the children that they can pray with their own words. I tried to repeat Greg's words, the words that he had taught them at the lessons. And then, I put questions to the classmates about what I had shared with them. Then some children put some questions to me. Then all of them were applauding to me. And you see it is so unusual in our school to applaud. Children never applaud to each other.

* * * * *

Greg: Dima, share how you came to know the Lord.

Dima: In August, I came to Jurmala for a weekend and met Greg Gulley and his team, the organization of New Life Ministries. We spent together only a few hours, but these few hours turned my life upside down. These hours were devoted to talks about Jesus Christ and for the first time in my life I learned what worship is and we sang together. I have always been interested in Jesus, but our Orthodox Church could never give me what I wanted.

Greg's team presented me with a Bible and a worshiping tape that I took home to Moscow. When I came home, and several days passed, a coup took place in the Soviet Union. For the first time in my life, I understood by myself what it means to have God in your heart, how God comes to people, and how He helps people. It was amazing.

On 20 August 1991, I left my house and went in the direction of the Russian White House to take part in defending the White House. I understood, as all people of good sense, that if we lose the government that we had at the time, we were going to lose everything. As I was walking in the direction of the White House, I suddenly heard one of the songs from the Hosanna tape, which I did not know by heart. At that moment, the words of the song—thanksgiving song—I could hear them in my head, and it seemed to me that it was without my will. Then I understood that it was Jesus who was bringing me to the White House, and it was Jesus who gave me the strength to go there. Then I understood quite clearly that nothing bad was going to happen.

The military dictatorship could not win in our country because God, who was bringing me to the barricades, was with us that night, with those who were defending the White House. I felt lightness in my heart. I understood that we were going to win in spite of the blood that was shed and the people killed.

Tanks were trying to attack the White House. But people who were there, people without weapons, just made a kind of chain in front of the tanks, and Jesus made those huge iron machines not come over the people who were supported by God. That was my first understanding of the will and love of Jesus.

Greg: So you were on the barricades, worshiping the Lord and praying all the time?

Dima: Yes, I was worshiping and praying because I was sure that only God could help us in this situation, only save us in this situation.

Greg: What did you hear about the impending attack? Did the government, via the radio, discourage people from going to the barricades, and if so, how much danger were you in?

Dima: Yes, the government tried to do this, but these were the leaders of the coup, and they tried to do their best to prevent people from going to the barricades. They did not tell directly that they were planning an attack. But we understood that all life of these people was in danger and they were trying to do their best to win their coup.

Greg: Now, Dima, going back to Jurmala, explain how you felt when you asked Jesus to come into your heart.

Dima: After I prayed to ask Jesus to come into my heart, I felt great joy and lightness. It seemed to me that I became better. It seemed to me that all those evil things that were in my life were passing away.

Greg: You accepted Christ during one of the performances. Explain the reaction of the children to the gospel.

Dima: That was wonderful because our children were watching the musicals. The members of the New Life team are extremely kind, and you can see this when they are on the stage because kindness is just radiating from their eyes.

Children are the most sensitive people on the whole planet. They are very sensitive to any falseness. It is impossible to deceive them. These children sat there watching the musicals with widely open eyes. I saw how in them the desire to be closer to the team was waking up, the desire to be closer to Jesus as the musicals were telling about Jesus, because I think that these unhappy children of our country have always lacked this belief. They have always lacked love that Jesus gives. They have always lacked the truth that is in Jesus. Their hearts wanted this, and they opened their hearts immediately, and Jesus came into their hearts. The team was a kind of conductor of Jesus into their hearts.

Greg: Now you mention the unhappiness of the children. Give us some insight into life in a Communist society and its impact upon the children.

Dima: You probably know, my dear friends, that seventy years of communism in my country have absolutely ruined the Soviet economy, but first of all the conscience of the people. I think that seventy years ago, devil came to our country in the form of the Com-

munist leaders and destroyed the country. The economy
is ruined; the conscience of people is ruined. All this led
to our children having nothing to eat, nothing to wear.
They cannot ask their mommies or daddies to buy toys
for them as we do not have any toys. That is terrible.
I think that during seventy years our children have
been living under these conditions, under these terrible conditions.

Plus the children have always been taught, beginning with kindergarten, to worship the devil in the
form of Lenin and Communist leaders. That is why
growing up the work of their minds was directed toward destroying and not building something. That is
why when I was watching the eyes of the children,
their radiating eyes—eyes that were taking in the kindness coming from the team members—I understood
that Jesus was coming into their hearts. It meant that
this generation may stop destroying and may begin
building when they grow up. That not the devil will
lead them in their lives but Jesus will take their hands
and guide them in their lives.

Greg: Growing up in Moscow, explain what you
were taught in the schools about Marxism-Leninism.

Dima: All childhood education in our country was
directed at only one thing—making of children people
who would strictly follow only the Communist ideals,
who should not differ from each other in any way, who
should be like mushrooms—one mushroom, another
mushroom, all the same. All the same growth and all
the same thickness. And children were begun to be
educated this way, even not at school, but when they
went to kindergarten. Children were also to be absolutely alike. Children should obey their nurses or teachers there. It could be compared with the system in the
army.

If somebody managed to see our alphabet, you could
see that even at the very first step when our children
were taught the alphabet, the first letters were about
their love for Lenin, their love for the Communist party.
When our children were having some holidays, they

used to sing songs only about Lenin, only about their love for the Communist party. And this thing continued in school.

The history was taught us through the prism of the Communist idea. History at our school was lie from the beginning to the very end. Now we know about this. History taught us what wonderful life our people have been having beginning with the revolution and up to the present. People of our country were having a wonderful, full life.

We were told how dangerous it is to live in the Capitalist countries. That these countries are full of poor, unemployed people. The children cannot go to school and lack all the things that our children have. You must understand now how mean the government that ruled us was to give us this impression of the world.

Very important thing at school was atheistic propaganda. People were told that what other people say about God is just a lie. Children were taught that only crazy people could believe in God. They made laugh of believers. And people took it all in since childhood.

Now the adults in their fifties, sixties, and seventies find it difficult to change their lives, to change themselves. It is difficult for them to come to Jesus now.

Greg: Since glasnost and perestroika, what have the people of the Commonwealth learned about Marxism-Leninism?

Dima: People learned all these terrible things that have taken place in our country since the October Revolution. People managed to read many literary works which describe the system, which were prohibited before, all our life. People managed to read secret documents which were signed by Lenin, Stalin, and their supporters. The documents in which Lenin approved of ruining the churches and in which Lenin approved bandit robbery of the churches. People managed to read the documents where Lenin signed his approval of shooting people. And the idea of Lenin being a grandpa was ruined.

Greg: Please share about the current situation in your country.

Dima: Taking into account the words of the leaders, everything is developing in the direction of capitalism. But it is not this way in reality. The leaders of our policy and economy, practically all of them, used to be the leaders of the Communist party in their past years. I think that some of them absolutely sincerely want to change the political and economic situation in the country. But I truly think that a person who has been propagating all his life and who has been studying all his life a Communist idea, and the idea occupies the most part of his mind, could hardly have fully cleansed his mind from the Communist ideas and turned in the direction of capitalism. It is much more difficult to turn from dictatorship to democracy than vice versa.

Now the situation with the prices being raised ten times and the salaries raised twice or three times leads to people being ready to vote for any leader who promises, at least promises, to give them some food and to lower the prices, to give them some clothes, to provide them with minimum of what they need for existing.

A new Russian party of the Bolsheviks is very active now. The ideas of national socialism and fascism are very popular among young people. These two movements are different in some ways, but in some things they are very close to each other. Both of them want to overthrow the democratic government, and the situation in the country is very unstable. And I think that nobody can predict what is going to happen with us in half a year, a year.

Then I think that the leaders of our country, the leaders of the ministries who are putting into life their forms of the government, are corrupted from the very beginning to the end. Our economy, the development of business in our country, is based on bribery. That is why many talented businessmen who could develop capitalism in our country, lacking the initial capital for giving briberies, just cannot start their business.

Greg: Is there real danger of the Communist party's taking power again?

Dima: Yes!

Greg: Explain briefly.

Dima: Why I think that the Communist regime can come to power is that some ten to fifteen years ago people lived a little better and got more material benefits than they get now. It was very primitive because they had very primitive clothes, and all the food was infected with different chemicals. But people did not know about this, and we were rather calm. Besides, ten to fifteen years ago, the government policy was to poison their people with vodka, to make them forget the reality by drinking.

Then the notorious Iron Curtain that prevented us from learning about the lives of other countries made us believe that we lived not worse than other countries, and our propaganda tried to assure us that we were living much better. And so now the majority of the population is sure that it will not be that bad if we could turn back to old times now. And so, anti-Yeltsin demonstrations are taking place now. And their slogans, which people are carrying, have the following words, "Give us bread!" So there is real danger of Communists coming back to power.

Greg: Dima, explain why the work of New Life Ministries and other Christian mission groups is crucial to the future of your country.

Dima: I think that what New Life Ministries is doing is just wonderful. I think that Jesus sends them to do what they are doing now. Because our country, in spite of the thing that religion is free now, the leading church in Russia is the Orthodox Church. They are Christians. We can say that they are Christians, but I think that what they are doing is not quite right. It is not enough, and it is not what God wants them to do because it seems to me that the main concern of the church is rebuilding of ruined churches and building new churches. All contribution of people is directed to rebuilding of old churches and building new churches.

I think that the main thing they should do now is forget about what they are to build or rebuild, but go to the people and not wait till the people come to the church. Go to the people themselves, what New Life Ministries is doing.

Here I see many letters the ministry gets from children and adults. I could see how inspired the people of my country were by meeting Greg Gulley and the team and how they are waiting for them to come back to my country. These are absolutely charming letters and one could read them with a smile. You could feel how children are trying to do their best, how reading the Bible they try to find the answers—answers to the questions that they are to answer and maybe the questions that they have in their lives. This way they memorize, and the words of the gospel come to their hearts.

13

As thou did send me into the world, I also have sent them into the world.

(John 17:18)

The Heart and Call of God

I vividly remember gazing out of my hotel window at the snow gently falling on the last night I spent in Moscow in November 1991. Packed bags rested against the wall, ready for the next day's flight back to America. In my briefcase were letters of invitation that secured more opportunities than I could have imagined. The previous seven days were an adventure. This trip took me to Riga and then to Moscow to follow up on inquiries we had received from our first three trips to the Soviet Union.

Sergei was able to arrange meetings for us with the Minister of Education of Latvia, Adris Pielbalgs; the Minister of Culture of Latvia, Raimonds Pauls; the Deputy Minister of Education of Russia, E.B. Courkins; the Deputy Minister of Culture of Russia, Nina Zhukova; and the directors of three children's hospitals. The United States Senator Jesse Helms graciously agreed to write a letter of introduction and recommendation to each of these prominent government leaders. The impending result of these meetings emphasized again the incredible place of history at which we stood as doors flew open wider than ever.

Those meetings resulted in invitations to evangelize, disciple, and distribute Christian literature and Bibles in any of Latvia's 889 schools and its theaters, and Russia's 64,581 traditional schools, representing 19,217,168 students, and its theaters.

As my heart stirred anew, December 1991 and January 1992 became a season of great reflection. We prayed and planned toward walking through those doors. Where do you begin? I prayed for more laborers. The harvest is plentiful.

All four of our teams would join us at the home office for Discipleship/Rehearsal Camp in January and February of the new year. We were blessed to welcome back a core of twelve veterans, and twelve new people would begin their journeys with us.

So much had happened. God unfolded such deep conviction in the closing months of 1991. How could I effectively share all that was on my heart? Could the baton of burden and vision be diligently passed, as Paul wrote to Timothy, "The things you have heard from me in the presence of many witnesses, these entrust to faithful men who would be able to teach others also?" (2 Tim. 2:2). Would this fire that burned within me burn with a passion within those who would begin the preparation to fulfill the first critical steps of God's vision here?

I was praying for God's theme for this Discipleship/Rehearsal Camp—our twenty-second here at New Life Ministries. Quickly, the answer to those prayers came. The Father's heart, His mission, His call would be our theme. So armed, I began to pray and study, not fully aware that this would be the most revolutionary, life-changing study I had ever undertaken.

The teams gathered in a conference room in a local hotel on 15 January 1992. With notes and heart prepared as best I knew how, I walked to the podium and opened with the following monologue—a short dramatic piece I wrote to illustrate the necessary ground rules for such a search. It set us all on a journey together, looking through a fresh set of eyes as we considered the most important of questions: What is on the Father's heart? What is His call, His mission for you and me and His church?

Someone has just made a difference in my life. That's right. I've got this friend. Well I didn't like him at first, didn't realize he was a friend until I found out that what he had been telling me all along was true. He took quite a risk . . . a chance that I might not be his friend anymore. But I've realized that he is a true friend because he dared to tell me the truth no matter what I might think and do in response. What I'm trying to say is, I just prayed with him to ask Jesus to come into my heart . . . be my Lord and Savior . . . and now I want to be just like my friend. Funny thing, isn't it? I used to be offended, and now I want to be like him.

His life is different. He dares to be that way. He's really given his life to this thing, and he's really given up everything to follow Jesus. There are not many like him, sad to say. But if he hadn't taken the time, and made a difference with his life, well, I don't know where I'd be today.

Well, I really want to take this thing seriously . . . I want to know what God wants for my life. He's got a plan, you know. But where to start? I want to grow, but I want to study those critically important things, the top priority items . . . I guess I want to know what's most important on God's heart. What's the bottom line here? So here I am in the Christian bookstore looking for answers . . . but there are so many different teaching tapes and books here. All good subjects, but what's the most important thing on God's heart? We've got success and prosperity, word of faith, prayer and intercession, discipleship plain and simple, the feasts, marriage and family, getting along with others, the single life, managing your money, know what you believe, the power of prayer. . . . phew!

Where to begin . . . and all the books and music and . . . well, how about Christian radio? You can forget that. I'm totally confused . . . one guy preaches fifteen minutes on speaking in tongues, the next guy preaches on the errors in the first guy's message. One does fifteen minutes on baptism, the next on baptism in Jesus' name only. . . .

So you know what I decided to do? Don't tell any-
body, but I got this revolutionary idea that if I
wanted to find out what the bottom line is, what is
chief on God's heart, maybe I should read the Bible.
You think that would help?

In attempting to decide the direction of this study,
I consulted my Bible's concordance. To my surprise,
only two Scriptures speak of the heart of God. The first
is 1 Samuel 13:14, and the second is Acts 13:22. Both
references refer to David as a man after God's own
heart, but neither define His heart.

As I prayed and examined Scripture, God revealed
three insights. First, God does not define His heart
because it is unfathomable. It would be confining for
the omnipotent Father to define His heart in a few
sentences, phrases, or terms that our finite minds could
comprehend. Second, God does not define His heart in
one or two verses because it is evident throughout
Scripture. God's heart is reflected in the pages of His
Word—in the lives of His people, His interaction with
them, through the life and ministry of Jesus, and the
writings of His followers.

Finally, the third insight He revealed is that sharing your heart is an intimate undertaking. It is not
something you share with just anyone. If we were going to share our hearts with someone, we would not
walk out and pull an individual in off the street. We
would search out someone whom we could trust with
that intimacy. Inherent in sharing your heart is a trust,
an obligation. The individual with whom you share it
has a responsibility. Your sharing obligates that individual. He must now ask himself, "Okay, what am I
going to do with this trust?" How is he going to respond
to this intimacy? God wants to share His heart with
everyone, but He is only going to share it with those
who will respond to it, with those whom He can trust
with the intimacy.

As we began to search the Scriptures in light of
these truths, some thought-provoking questions surfaced. What if God does begin to reveal His heart to us?

What if, in the process of revealing His heart to us, God also unfolds before us our own hearts, their condition, and how they line up or don't line up with His heart? Dare we take that risk, the risk of being challenged to choose to allow Him to change our hearts? What if we do seek God's heart and God's call, and what if God begins to reveal His heart and call to us? How will we be obligated then? Is it better not to know? What is the work of God? What is He seeking to accomplish on earth?

I began to search the Scriptures, beginning with the Gospels. My theme was God's heart, mission, and call. I found over one hundred verses that speak of these themes in the gospels alone. I surveyed the rest of the New Testament, Paul's epistles, the letters of Peter and John, and Revelation. It was all so overwhelming. Right before my eyes in plain view was the heart and call of God echoed again and again, on every page, in every divine action. How could I have been so blind? Had I refused to see, consumed with God's meeting my own needs and not about what was on His heart, always ready to pour out my heart before His throne, with not a thought as to what burdened Him?

This survey revolutionized my thinking on missions. It truly gripped me. Missions is not an option; it is a mandate. It is not secondary on God's heart; it is primary. Missions is not an arm of the church; it is an expression of our identity. It is not what the church does, but who the church is. If the body of Christ is not fulfilling this commission, due to disobedience or ignorance, then we are not expressing who we are—our essential character. We are no less called to fulfill the commission of Christ than the first twelve apostles or Paul.

God is a missionary God, clearly stating His mission in the Bible, a truly missionary book. The Bible emphatically gives us a missions mandate. It unequivocally "shouts" to all those who call themselves followers of Jesus Christ to become missionaries like their missionary Father and His missionary Son.

Jesus said, "As the Father has sent me, I also send you" (John 20:21). Sending is an action. It demands movement. To be sent rather than to just go demands a dependency on the Sender by the sent as well as total obedience and complete surrender to His mission. It requires relinquishing your will to the mission and call of God. Jesus, as our example, was totally dependent on the Father. He did only what He saw the Father doing, and He did it in like manner (John 5:19). He depended on the Father to set Him apart and fully prepare Him. Additionally, he relied on the Father to prepare the way, to equip, to send, and to work through Him.

How did Jesus place Himself in a position where God could fully use Him? He gave up all; He emptied Himself. He laid down His life for others. His food was to do the will of His Father—to accomplish His work (John 4:34). He lived a life of consummate obedience to God's call, a life fully given to being the Word and preaching the Word. God sent Jesus "to seek and to save that which was lost" (Luke 19:10). Jesus passes the baton to us: "And you shall be my witnesses" (Acts 1:8).

How Serious is God Anyway?

The first evidence we see of God's seriousness in this mission and call is the history of His dealings with His people. It helps us to gain true perspective when we consider what I call the "reality of the extremes." In creation, and through the garden, God went to the extreme to wonderfully and excellently create the world. He lovingly went to the extreme in giving Adam and Eve absolutely everything they needed physically, emotionally, and spiritually to abundantly live and prosper.

But how did they respond to God's expression of extreme love, provision, blessing, and sacrifice? They responded with extreme rebellion. No, man's rebellion is not passive. Not only do we go our own way and turn our backs on God, as if that is not bad enough, but we even begin to deny He exists, living our lives and building society based on that denial. Our self-centeredness, selfishness, and base sin actively seek to factor the Creator of the universe out of every aspect of His creation. The world man seeks to create proves this phenomenon. Virtually every society cleaves to a philosophy that places man at the center of the universe as the means and end of every thought, word, and deed.

God had every reason to wash His hands of man after his rebellion. But He did not. Man fell, and God repeatedly reached out. Throughout the pages of the Bible, we witness God's going to extremes to reach a rebellious people. He compassionately employed every means He deemed necessary, sending judges, kings, prophets, and finally His only Son.

Jesus told a parable that parallels His Father's efforts through history (Luke 20:9-18):

> A man planted a vineyard and rented it out to vine-growers, and went on a journey for a long time. And at the harvest time he sent a slave to the vine-growers, in order that they might give him some of the produce of the vineyard; but the vine-growers beat him and sent him away empty-handed. And he proceeded to send another slave; and they beat him also and treated him shamefully, and sent him away empty-handed. And he proceeded to send a third; and this one also they wounded and cast out. And the owner of the vineyard said, "What shall I do? I will send my beloved son; perhaps they will respect him." But when the vine-growers saw him, they reasoned with one another, saying, "This is the heir; let us kill him that the inheritance may be ours." And they cast him out of the vineyard and killed him. What, therefore, will the owner of the vineyard do to them? He will come and destroy these vine-growers and will give the vineyard to others.

> And when they heard it, they said, "May it never be." But He looked at them and said, "What then is

this that is written, 'The stone which the builders rejected, this became the chief cornerstone'? Every one who falls on that stone will be broken to pieces; but on whomever it falls, it will scatter him like dust."

Here in this parable Jesus is recalling God's efforts to reach man again and restore mankind to Himself. It is no coincidence that the three slaves line up numerically with God's efforts throughout history to reach out to His people. When His disciples heard this parable, they said, "May it never be." The Chief Cornerstone stood in their midst, recounting what had already taken place, echoing God's seriousness, His efforts. And the disciples said, "May it never be." They missed the point. It already *was,* and Jesus stood before them as the fulfillment of the story.

In Jesus' life and death, we see the second indication of God's seriousness. "For God so loved the world, that He gave His only begotten Son, that whoever believes in Him should not perish, but have eternal life." As I've stated before, God was not obligated in any way, shape, or fashion to step in again and make a way for all men to be reconciled to Him. But He did. God again, out of His extreme love and mercy, went to the extreme in reaching out once more. He made the ultimate sacrifice in the midst of man's rebellion and gives His own Son, Jesus, an extreme sacrifice for a people in absolute rebellion. In Philippians 2:5-8, we read of what Jesus gave up to meet our need:

> Have this attitude in yourselves which was also in Christ Jesus, who, although He existed in the form of God did not regard equality with God a thing to be grasped, but emptied Himself, taking the form of a bond-servant, and being made in the likeness of men. And being found in appearance as a man, He humbled Himself by becoming obedient to the point of death, even death on a cross.

What Jesus gave up for us and then suffered echoes the seriousness of God. He emptied Himself. He gave of

Himself in the way that would most benefit man. He became a man and ultimately suffered the cruelest of deaths for us. Isaiah prophesied of the suffering servant who would pay it all.

> He was despised and rejected by men, a man of sorrows, and familiar with suffering. Like one from whom men hide their faces he was despised, and we esteemed Him not. . . . He was oppressed and afflicted, yet He did not open his mouth; He was led like a lamb to the slaughter, and as a sheep before the shearers is silent, so He did not open His mouth. (Isa. 53:3, 7)

We had turned our backs on God. "There is none righteous, not even one; there is none who understands, there is none who seeks God. All have turned aside, together they have become useless; there is none who does good, there is not even one" (Rom. 3:10-12). But while our backs were still turned in extreme rebellion, God gave His beloved Son that we might be reconciled to Him.

> For while we were still helpless, at the right time Christ died for the ungodly. For one will hardly die for a righteous man; though perhaps for the good man someone would dare even to die. But God demonstrates His own love toward us, in that while we were yet sinners, Christ died for us. (Rom. 5:6-8)

In response, what does Jesus demand of those who wish to follow Him? What does He require in response to His extreme sacrifice—the giving of His life? What does God ask of us in light of this expression of His extreme love? Nothing less than extreme commitment.

Jesus said, "If any man wills to come after Me, let him deny himself [that is forsake, lose sight of himself and his own interests], take up his cross daily and follow Me [that is, cleave steadfastly to Me, conform wholly to My example, in living, and if need be in dying also]" (Luke 9:23).

The third evidence of God's seriousness in reaching out to the world is underlined in "The Great Commis-

sion" (Matt. 28:18-20). Obviously, we hear the part
directed toward us—the "go" portion. Unfortunately,
we may miss an equally important impetus that makes
our "going" possible if we pass over verse 18.

When I was studying those verses, God impressed
upon my heart that I needed to back up. I was missing
something. Carefully, I examined verse 18, which reads,
"Then Jesus came to them and said, 'All authority in
heaven and on earth has been given to Me.'"

Here is Jesus, God's faithful Son, pure and without
sin. Throughout His ministry, He listened to the Father, did only what He saw the Father doing, and did
it in like manner. "I tell you the truth, the Son can do
nothing by Himself; He can do only what He sees His
Father doing, because whatever the Father does the
Son also does" (John 5:19). He was a faithful steward
over all the tasks His Father gave Him. Here He stands
with the power of heaven in His hand. In what is this
faithful steward going to invest all the authority of
heaven and earth bestowed upon Him? How shall He
focus His energy and authority?

God's Son can do nothing less than reflect the priority of heaven. He is not going to depart from the
pattern He followed throughout His ministry. He is
going to look to the Father and reflect the Father's
heart in His investment.

What are the next words uttered by Jesus? "Therefore go and make disciples of all nations, baptizing
them in the name of the Father and of the Son and of
the Holy Spirit, and teaching them to obey everything
I have commanded you. And surely I am with you
always, to the very end of the age" (Matt. 28:19-20).

The energy and agenda of heaven is poured into the
Great Commission. He did not invest the authority of
heaven and earth in making us happy, comfortable,
Sunday morning Christians, all behatted and begloved
in piety. He invested it for the discipling of nations.
Heaven's number one priority is proclaimed. God's
agenda is revealed. Is there any doubt about what is
foremost in His heart?

A fourth evidence is His reason for sending us the Holy Spirit. We see it in Acts 1:8. The resurrected Jesus says to His apostles, "But you will receive power when the Holy Spirit comes on you; and you will be My witnesses in Jerusalem, and in all Judea and Samaria, and to the ends of the earth." He invests the power of the Holy Spirit in these men and in each one of us so we can . . . wait for the sweet by and by? No! He invested the power of the Holy Spirit in these men and in us so we could be His "witnesses in Jerusalem, and in all Judea and Samaria, and to the ends of the earth." Echoing the priority of heaven, He invested the power of the Holy Spirit, anointing these men for service.

John R. W. Stott wrote of our mandate in *Perspectives*:

> The Bible gives us the mandate for world evangelization. We certainly need one. Our mandate for world evangelization therefore is the whole Bible. It is to be found in the creation of God because of which all human beings are responsible to Him; and the character of God as outgoing, loving, compassionate, not willing that any should perish, desiring that all should come to repentance; and the promises of God that all nations will be blessed with Abraham's seed; and with the coming Messiah's inheritance; and the Christ of God now exalted with universal acclaim; and the Spirit of God who convicts of sin, witnesses of Christ and compels the church to evangelize; and the church of God, which is a multi-national missionary community under orders to evangelize until Christ returns. This global dimension of the Christian mission is irresistible. Individual Christians in local churches not committed to world evangelization are contradicting, either through blindness or disobedience, an essential part of their God-given identity. The Biblical mandate for world evangelization cannot be escaped.

The fifth evidence of God's seriousness is the reality of where one is without Christ. Without Christ, man is destined for hell. A person who is spiritually

lost is spiritually dead and a resident of the domain of
darkness. He is at the devil's mercy. He is separated
from God and destined for eternal damnation. "And
you were dead in your trespasses and sins, in which
you formerly walked according to the course of this
world, according to the prince of the power of the air,
of the spirit that is now working in the sons of disobedience" (Eph. 2:1-2).

But in His infinite mercy, God delivered us from
certain destruction. "But God being rich in mercy, because of His great love with which He loved us, even
when we were dead in our transgressions, made us
alive together with Christ" (Eph. 2:4-5). "For He delivered us from the domain of darkness, and transferred
us to the kingdom of His beloved Son, in whom we have
redemption, the forgiveness of sins" (Col. 1:13-14). Jesus
understood the condition of mankind. He did not approach His mission as a hobby. He understood man's
hopelessness so deeply that He was willing to do anything and everything to remedy the situation, even
dying on a cross.

We so easily lose sight of the reality of eternity, the
reality of spending eternity in hell, separated from
God. It is crucial that we regain the revelation of what
it is to be lost. We cannot remain complacent about the
truth. If we embrace the condition of man apart from
Christ, it will fuel the urgency of giving our lives before
the throne to see every man, woman, and child rescued
from that sentence. Jim Elliot wrote, "May we who
know Christ hear the cry of the damned as they hurdle
headlong into the Christless night without ever a
chance. May we shed tears of repentance for those we
failed to bring out of the darkness."

Are We Answering the Call?

As a strong river flows down its logical course, so I
was pulled to the next logical, honest step of self-ex-
amination. We are now face-to-face with God's heart,
call, and mission. Is the body of Christ responding?

Have we heeded God's call? Look with me at some staggering statistics.

Worldwide, the Christian church can only boast 85,000 full-time missionaries out of more than 400,000 churches. A statistic from *Global Prayer Digest* revealed that ninety percent of those who say they are called to the mission field never go. If we simply tithed the memberships of our churches in America, we would more than quadruple the current number in the field. Consider this pathetic number against the need. Over 2.5 billion people have never heard the gospel. Yet, only 5,000 to 7,000 missionaries worldwide work with these unreached groups—one missionary for every 450,000 people. Over 16,000 distinct cultures and groups have not one Christian church. Over 5,199 languages have no Bible or Scripture translations. Over 80,000 unsaved people die every day.

Now that we are aware of our dismal response to God's heart, wholly ignoring His agenda as evidenced by the statistics and facts presented here, can we rejoice at all in how we give our resources to His work? No!

Americans give $700 million annually to missions. Sound impressive? Not when one considers that we spend the same amount on chewing gum in a year or on pet food in fifty-two days. Americans will spend that much on suntan lotion in little more than a year, monies given at the altar of the "sun god" rather than in worship of the Son of the Living God. If you give more than $1.50 on missions monthly, you are spending more than ninety percent of the Christians in this nation. It is shameful to confront the reality of our materialism and decadence. Adding insult to injury is our notion that we have done a good job in this nation of responding to God's heart and mission to reach the world.

How are church budgets lining up with God's heart? Dr. Ralph Winter of the Center for World Mission has developed an evangelism chart to demonstrate how the local church spends its money in response to the Great Commission. He found that ninety-five percent of the

churches' monies are allotted to E-0 and E-1 evangelism. E-0 is evangelism with "0" barriers. It is evangelism that takes place within the four walls of the church.
E-1 stands for evangelism that takes place outside the
church, but close by. In other words, we are spending
ninety-five percent on ourselves. Only four-and-a-half
percent of the local church's money is allotted for E-3
through E-5 evangelism, reaching across cultural, language, geographical, and political barriers. Moreover,
only one-half percent goes to unreached people groups.

These numbers dispel any notions that we are
meeting our obligations financially. Obviously, we, as
the body of Christ in America, need to examine our
priorities. We need to get in touch with the heart and
call of God. Through ignorance or disobedience, we
have distanced ourselves from our mission. It is not
that God needs us. He blesses us by allowing us to
participate in His plan. But we have to be willing to
respond. God gave us life, and we are challenged to
invest it in those endeavors that will reap eternal divi-
dends.

In June 1992, the Blue Team and I boarded a bus
in Sochi, Russia, a city on the Black Sea, to travel to
our next outreach in the Sochi Children's Hospital.
Joining us was a news reporter from the Sochi newspaper. She was assigned to do a feature story on our
team.

It was a candid interview, giving me the opportunity to share the heart of what we do. Her last question
put into perspective what I am discussing here. In
asking about the reason we share the gospel, she inquired as to whether evangelism was traditional for
Americans or built into our culture. Sadly, I had to
explain that missions is a complete diversion from cultural or traditional norms. On the contrary, we would
be considered a cultural anomaly.

Why Are We Failing?

The next logical questions are "Why are we failing
so miserably at searching out God's heart and answer-

ing His call? Why do ninety percent of those called fail to follow through?" My initial reaction was that maybe they were never called in the first place. But if that were the case, then Jesus would not have said, "The harvest is plentiful but the workers are few. Therefore beseech the Lord of the harvest to send out workers into His harvest" (Matt. 9:37-38).

No, many are called, but they face an enemy—the enemy of their souls—whose purpose is to obstruct the will of God. Satan strives to see that we do anything but seek after God's will and then respond to His call. Obviously, he does not want us to be Christ's vessels of love to a lost and dying world. His goal is to spiritually, physically, and emotionally destroy as many as possible. Satan will exhaust every means to prevent people from proclaiming God's truth to those who are shackled in the chains and bondage of his kingdom of darkness.

One way that he discourages workers is by making us feel as though we are fighting an uphill battle that can never be won. He gives us the impression that working in the mission field is like fighting a 100,000 -acre forest fire with a water pistol and the wind against us. He lies to us and tells us that one person cannot make a difference. We become discouraged when we look at the vast need and fall prey to his falsehoods.

We must recognize Satan's deceit. One life does make a difference when surrendered to the omnipotent Father. It is the ripple effect of discipling individuals that is truly incomprehensible. Jesus spent most of His ministry discipling twelve men. Look at the fruit.

Mary's daughter, Tanya, is another example of this ripple effect. We touched Tanya's life, and she in turn shared with thirty individuals in her public school classroom.

Our lack of a missions conviction in the churches of America is another stumbling block. Developing a conviction first takes an awareness, and we are not aware of God's missions mandate in Scripture. Moreover, it seems that we do not care to be aware. The church must wake up to the fact that God is a missionary God. He has given us a missionary mandate. Then that head knowledge must invade our hearts. An awareness will not get the job done. We must embrace the call.

The church in America acts as if Christ saved us from a sprained ankle or a hangnail. As Keith Green wrote before his death, "Hell is not for the weekend." It is as if the condition of mankind, the desperation, the hopelessness, the hell destination is all myth. If it were real to us, there would be more fervent activity. Someone is screaming from the second floor of a burning house. Not only do you see him, but you have a ladder. You are carrying the means to rescue him. How long would you ponder the call? You see someone standing in the path of an oncoming train. How long would you debate the merits of your present life in light of the call? How long would you pore over Scriptures to make sure you should warn that person or even push him out of the way? We debate because we do not fully embrace the fate from which Jesus saved us. Amy Carmichael once wrote, "Satan is so much more in earnest than we are. He is buying up every opportunity, while we are still counting the cost." Our prayer should not be, "God, should I go?" but "God, why shouldn't I go?"

Through ignorance and disobedience, we have so distanced ourselves from the mission field that we rarely hear of a church member who answers the call. And if God kindles something in the heart of an individual in a congregation, frequently he is not encouraged by the local church or the witness of the people around him. In many cases, he is looked upon as a person who could not find a real job, so he's thinking about missions. How pathetic to think that we have so diminished God's mandate to reach the lost that many think of it as a task for those who could find nothing better to do. America has been truly blessed. But like the Dead Sea, we have not been the channel of blessing to others that God intended us to be. We are loved so that we might love. We are saved so that we might share Christ with others.

The time has come, and is indeed long overdue, for individuals and the church to search the Word of God. We need to make it the standard and judge the legitimacy of every church task and expenditure in light of its truths—in light of its revelation of God's heart and call to "go into all the world and preach the Gospel to all creation" (Mark 16:15).

This process begins with the recognition that our cultural mores obscure the call of God. In light of this recognition, we need to go to the Word and go before the Father, asking some provocative questions. What does Scripture reveal about God's call on the individual and the church? After all, if we are to follow in His steps, what was Jesus' mission on earth? What did He call His disciples to do? How did that call flesh out in the lives of these men? Did they surrender to His call with qualifications, or did they obey without reservation?

Taking a hard look in the mirror, we need to probe further. Knowing God's heart and call to His harvest fields, how will we respond to Him? Do our established priorities line up with His call? How has American culture affected our response? To what extent am I willing to step out and obey Him, no matter the cost? What right does He have over my life? Dare we ask these questions? Dare we risk answering the call? John Wesley once said, "Give me men who hate nothing but sin and love nothing but God and I will win England."

What will you do now, simply be more "aware," but do nothing in response? I beg you, do not let another minute pass before you deal, individually, one-on-one, with God's calling on your life. Are you living your life the way God intended? When you stand before His throne, will Jesus say to you, "Well done, thou good and faithful servant"?

Bibliography for Chapter IV

Barry, Donald D. and Barner-Barry, Carol. *Contemporary Soviet Politics*. Englewood Cliffs, New Jersey: Prentice-Hall, Inc., 1982.

Buss, Gerald. *The Bear's Hug*. Grand Rapids, Michigan: W.B. Eerdsman Publishing Company, 1987.

Hindus, Maurice. *Humanity Uprooted*. New York, New York: Jonathon Cape and Harrison Smith, Inc., 1929.

Redl, Helen B., ed. *Soviet Educators on Soviet Education*. New York, New York: Free Press of Glencoe, 1964.

Skousen, W. Cleon. *The Naked Communist*. Salt Lake City, Utah: The Ensign Publishing Company, 1961.

Solzhenitsyn, Aleksandr Isayevich. *Gulag Archipelago I, II, and III*. New York, New York: Harper and Row, 1973.

MORE GOOD BOOKS FROM
HUNTINGTON HOUSE PUBLISHERS

RECENT RELEASES

America: Awaiting the Verdict
by Mike Fuselier

We are a nation stricken with an infectious disease. The disease is called betrayal—we are a nation that has denied, rejected, and betrayed our Christian past. The symptoms of the disease are many and multiplying daily. Mike Fuselier thus encourages Americans to return to the faith of their founding fathers—the faith upon which our law and government rests—or suffer the consequences. To prove that our forebearers were in no way attempting to establish a secular state, as contended by secular humanists, the author presents oft-forgotten but crucial evidence to fortify his—and all Christians'—case.

ISBN 1-56384-034-0 $5.99

Battle Plan: Equipping the Church for the 90s
by Chris Stanton

Already into the nineties and it's easy to see that the institutions of American society—the family, the church, the government—will continue to look little like the same entities of all prior decades! The evidences have been discussed before. Now is the time to talk about why and what to do about it. A new battle plan is needed. The author dissects the characteristics of the enemy and the effectiveness of its attacks on the church. Then he lays out the military strategy for the spiritual warriors of the 1990s. The enemy won't know what hit him if the Church diligently readies itself for this all-important battle!

ISBN 1-56384-034-0 $7.99

Don't Touch That Dial:
The Impact of the Media on Children and the Family
by Barbara Hattemer & Robert Showers

Men and women without any stake in the outcome of the war between the pornographers and our families have come to the qualified, professional agreement that media does have an effect on our children—an effect that is devastatingly significant. Highly respected researchers, psychologists, and sociologists join the realm of pediatricians, district attorneys, parents, teachers, pastors, and community leaders—who have diligently remained true to the fight against filthy media—in their latest comprehensive critique of the modern media establishment (i.e., film, television, print, art, curriculum).

ISBN Quality Trade Paper   1-56384-032-4 $9.99
ISBN Hardcover 1-56384-035-9 $19.99

En Route to Global Occupation
by Gary Kah

High-ranking government liaison Gary Kah warns that national sovereignty will soon be a thing of the past. Invited to join the WCPA (World Constitution and Parliamentary Association), the author was involved in the planning and implementation of a one-world government. For the skeptical observer, the material in this book "should serve as ample evidence that the drive to create a one-world government is for real." Reproductions of the original documentation are included.

ISBN 0-910311-97-8 $9.99

Face the Wind
by Gloria Delaney

Thoughts of suicide, abuse, rape, drugs, booze, tattoos, jail, anger, hatred, revenge, and depression marked the endless cycle of the author's life as Speedy, an unloved teen-ager and "motorcycle old lady;" she was the possession of Crazy Nick. When she discovered that she was pregnant and felt the baby first move within her, panic turned to determination. Little Michael was born, and, through the vile corruption of life with Crazy, Gloria clung to the beauty of motherhood and the innocence of her child, committing herself to his welfare above all else. Read about her escape with Michael and how she found the One who would lift her out of her past and make her wholly clean. This book celebrates motherhood and demonstrates how the miracle of new life can point the lost to the Author of Life.

ISBN 1-56384-011-1 $9.99

False Security:
Has the New Age Given Us a False Hope?
by Jerry Parks

The Great Tribulation! Wars, famine, pestilence, persecution—these are just some of the frightful events in the future of the world. Are they in your future? For centuries, the prophets searched the Scriptures for the timing of the first coming of the Messiah, now we watch and wait for the Second Coming of Christ and everything that foreshadows it. In *False Security: Has the New Age Given Us a False Hope?* author Jerry Parks discusses a relatively recent teaching that has infiltrated the Church, giving many a false hope. When will the Rapture occur? Be prepared to examine your own beliefs and clear up many of the questions you may have about the close of this age.

ISBN 1-56384-012-X $9.99

A Jewish Conservative Looks at Pagan America
by Don Feder

With eloquence and insight that rival contemporary commentators and essayists of antiquity, Don Feder's pen finds his targets in the enemies of God, family, and American tradition and morality. Deftly ... delightfully ... the master allegorist and Titan with a typewriter brings clarity to the most complex sociological issues and invokes giggles and wry smiles from both followers and foes. Feder is Jewish to the core, and he finds in his Judaism no inconsistency with an American Judeo-Christian ethic. Questions of morality plague school administrators, district court judges, senators, congressmen, parents, and employers; they are wrestling for answers in a "changing world." But Feder challenges the evolving society theory and directs inquirers to the original books of wisdom: the Torah and the Bible

ISBN Quality Trade Paper 1-56384-036-7$9.99
ISBN Hardcover 1-56384-037-5 $19.99

Journey into Darkness: Nowhere to Land
by Stephen L. Arrington

This story begins on Hawaii's glistening sands and ends in the mysterious deep with the Great White Shark. In between he found himself trapped in the drug smuggling trade—unwittingly becoming the "Fall Guy" in the highly publicized John Z. DeLorean drug case. Naval career shattered, his youthful innocence tested, and friends and family put to the test of loyalty, Arrington locked on one Truth during his savage stay in prison and endeavors to share that critical truth now. Focusing on a single important message to young people—to stay away from drugs—the author recounts his horrifying prison experience and allows the reader to take a peek at the source of hope and courage that helped him survive.

ISBN 1-56384-003-3 $9.99

Political Correctness:
The Cloning of the American Mind
by David Thibodaux, Ph.D.

The author, professor of literature at the University of Southwestern Louisiana, confronts head on the movement that is now being called Political Correctness. Political Correctness, says Thibodaux, "is an umbrella under which advocates of civil rights, gay and lesbian rights, feminism, and environmental causes have gathered." To incur the wrath of these groups, one only has to disagree with them on political, moral, or social issues. To express traditionally Western concepts in universities today can result in not only ostracism, but even suspension. (According to a recent "McNeil-Lehrer News Hour" report, one student was suspended for discussing the reality of the moral law with an avowed homosexual. He was reinstated only after he apologized.)

ISBN Quality Trade Paper 1-56384-026-X $9.99
ISBN Hardcover 1-56384-033-2 $18.99

The Subtle Serpent:
New Age in the Classroom
by Darylann Whitemarsh & Bill Reisman

There is a new morality being taught to our children in public schools. Without the consent or even awareness of parents—educators and social engineers are aggressively introducing new moral codes to our children. In most instances, these new moral codes contradict the traditional values. Darylann Whitemarsh (a 1989 Teacher of the Year) and Bill Reisman (educator and expert on the occult) combine their knowledge to expose the deliberate madness occurring in our public schools.

ISBN 1-56384-016-2 $9.99

Touching the Face of God
by Bob Russell

This book chronicles the spiritual odyssey of Bob Russell—author, pilot, super-salesman, Christian philosopher. It is the gripping account of one man's love affair with the sky and the obstacles he overcame to become one of America's best-known aviators. It is also the story of how he reaffirmed his faith in everything he did—and how his courage helped him to survive the heartbreaking loss of friends, children, and wife. The author notes his life from the Great Depression until the twilight of the Cold War. It is a true account of survival in the face of poverty and war and an intimate picture of love and marriage.

ISBN Quality Trade Paper 1-56384-010-3 $8.99
ISBN Hardcover 1-56384-015-4 $18.99

When the Wicked Seize a City
by Chuck & Donna McIlhenny with Frank York

A highly publicized lawsuit . . . a house fire-bombed in the night . . . the shatter of windows smashed by politically (and wickedly) motivated vandals cuts into the night . . . All because Chuck McIlhenny voiced God's condemnation of a behavior and life-style and protested the destruction of society that results from its practice. That behavior is homosexuality, and that life-style is the gay culture. This book explores: the rise of gay power and what it will mean if Christians do not organize and prepare for the battle; homosexual attempts to have the American Psychiatric Association remove pedophilia from the list of mental illnesses—now they want homophobia declared a disorder.

ISBN 1-56384-024-3 $9.99

You Hit Like a Girl
by Elsa Houtz & William J. Ferkile

Rape—it's the issue that dominates the headlines. Have things changed since the days when women and children were afforded respect and care by all members of society? What does self-protection mean in the 1990s in this age of higher rates of violent crime and the "progressiveness" of the women's movement? What can women do to protect themselves? What can men do to protect the women they love—or the children they'd sacrifice their very lives to shelter from harm? The authors, self-defense experts, have developed a thorough guide to self-protection that addresses the mental attitude of common sense safety and details the practical means by which women can protect themselves and their children.

ISBN 1-56384-031-6 $9.99

The Blessings of Liberty: Restoring the City on the Hill
by Charles Heath

The author believes Liberalism is destroying our nation. If we continue to do nothing, says Heath, the traditional family values that we cherish and the kind of government envisioned by our founding fathers will cease to exist. Heath presents a coherent case for limited government, decentralized and self-governing communities, and a return to traditional values. Conservatism, he continues, has its premise in the book of Genesis. It is the only viable philosophy capable of addressing and solving today's problems.

ISBN Quality Trade Paper 1-56384-005-7 $8.99

One Year to a College Degree
by Lynette Long & Eileen Hershberger

College: Anyone who's been through the gauntlet of higher education's administrative red tape can attest to the frustration and confusion that accompanies the process. Twenty-eight years after a failed first semester, co-author Eileen Hershberger embarked on the admirable, albeit frightening venture, as an adult learner. One year later she earned her bachelor's degree. With Lynette Long, she reveals the secret in this thorough self-help book, complete with reference guide, work sheets, and resource lists. Most intriguing are the inside tips only professors and upper-level counselors would know.

ISBN 1-56384-001-4 $9.99

Hitler and the New Age
by Bob Rosio

Hail Caesar! Heil Hitler! Hail—who? Who will be next? Many recognize Caesar and Nero and Hitler as forerunners of the future, when one leader, backed by one government and religious church, will lead one worldwide system. The question is, Were they all tools to prepare the way for the very old and evil world order? Bob Rosio believes that studying an extreme type of historical figure, such as Hitler, will help Christians better understand and better prepare a battle plan to stand against the New Age movement and this emerging world order. He describes this book as "a study in the mechanics of evil."

ISBN 1-56384-009-X $9.99

Exposing the AIDS Scandal
by Dr. Paul Cameron

Where do you turn when those who control the flow of information in this country withhold the truth? Why is the national media hiding facts from the public? Can AIDS be spread in ways we're not being told? Finally, a book that gives you a total account for the AIDS epidemic, and what steps can be taken to protect yourself. What you don't know can kill you!

ISBN 0-910311-52-8 $7.99

NOVELS

Angel Vision
by Jim Carroll & Jay Gaines

Legends about the mysterious and beautiful Ozark mountains in Arkansas abound among the locals. Three men, strangers to one another, find themselves pitted against the evil housed deep within the Lost Louisiana Mine. Millionaire Walter Carson, Reverend Victor Peterson, and karate instructor Jason Howser are involved in separate accidents that leave each of them in a deep coma. Neither dead nor alive, the three awaken to meet their ghostly comrades and a mysterious stranger, Clay, who attempts to fuse them into a team of survivors and warriors for the Lord.

ISBN Mass Market Paperback 1-56384-006-5 $5.99

Legend of the Holy Lance
by Bill Still

From an awesome galactic rock the most mysterious weapons in history will be forged: The Holy Lance and Sword. These icons of power will become the symbols of conquerors: Saul, Nebuchadnezzar, Cyrus the Persian, Alexander the Great, Julius Caesar, Constantine, Attila the Hun, Merlin, Napoleon, and Hitler. The Lance was ensconced in museums, hidden in ice caves and castle walls, and raised to the status of holy relic as the purported spear that pierced the side of Christ. A career-hardened reporter and a beautiful Yale senior discover that the Lance is held by a secret society in Germany and find themselves catapulted into the realm of international conspiracy.

ISBN Quality Trade Paper 1-56384-002-2 $8.99
ISBN Hardcover 1-56384-008-1 $16.99

Cover of Darkness
by J. Carroll

Jack's time is running out. The network's top investigative reporter has been given the most bizarre and difficult assignment of his life. The powers behind a grand conspiracy (occult and demonic forces) are finally exposed by Jack. Now comes the real challenge—convincing others. Matching wits with supernatural forces, Jack faces the most hideous conspiracy the world has ever known.

ISBN 0-910311-31-5 $7.99

Crystalline Connection
by Bob Maddux & Mary Carpenter Reid

Enter the enchanting world of Ebbern, a planet in many ways like our own. In the Crystalline Connection, our hero, Bracken, returns to his homeland after ten years of wandering. Once there he becomes involved in a monumental struggle gallantly confronting the dark forces of evil. This futuristic fantasy is fraught with intrigue, adventure, romance and much more. The Crystalline Connection artfully discloses the devastating consequences of involvement in the New Age movement while using the medium of fiction.

ISBN 0-910311-71-4 $8.99

THE SALT SERIES

Exposing the AIDS Scandal
by Paul Cameron, M.D.

AIDS is 100 percent fatal all of the time. There are believed to be over 1,500,000 people in the United States carrying the AIDS virus. The ever-growing number of cases compels us to question whether there will be a civilization in twenty years.

ISBN 1-56384-023-5 $2.99

Inside the New Age Nightmare
by Randall Baer

Are your children safe from the New Age movement? This former New Age leader, one of the world's foremost experts in crystals, brings to light the darkest of the darkness that surrounds the New Age movement. The week that Randall Baer's original book was released, he met with a puzzling and untimely death—his car ran off a mountain pass. His death is still regarded as suspicious.

ISBN 1-56384-022-7 $2.99

The Question of Freemasonry
by Ed Decker

Blood oaths, blasphemy, and illegal activity—in this day and age it's hard to believe these aberrations still exist; this booklet demonstrates that the Freemasons are not simply a "goodwill," community-oriented organization.

ISBN 1-56384-020-0 $2.99

To Moroni With Love
by Ed Decker

Readers are led through the deepest of the Mormon church doctrines and encouraged to honestly determine whether the words can be construed as heresy in light of the true, or as unadulterated language of the Bible. Decker reveals shocking material that has caused countless Mormon's to question the church leaders and abandon Mormonism's false teachings.

ISBN 1-56384-021-9 $2.99

Backlist/Best-sellers

America Betrayed
by Marlin Maddoux

This hard-hitting book exposes the forces in our country which seek to destroy the family, the schools, our culture, and our values. The author details exactly how the news media manipulates your mind. Maddoux is the host of the popular national radio talk show, "Point of View."

ISBN 0-910311-18-8 $6.99

Deadly Deception
by Jim Shaw & Tom McKenney

For the first time the 33 degree ritual is made public! Learn of the "secrets" and "deceptions" that are practiced daily around the world. Find out why Freemasonry teaches that it is the true religion, that all other religions are but corrupted and perverted forms of Freemasonry. If you know anyone in the Masonic movement, you must read this book.

ISBN 0-910311-54-4 $7.99

Delicate Balance
by John Zajac

Find out what forces in the universe are at work and why the earth is in a very delicate balance. The author displays his research to present the overall picture at hand that packages and interconnects economics, prophesy, ecology, militarism, and theology. Can modern science unlock the mysteries of the future? Can we determine our own fate or are we part of a larger scheme beyond our control?

ISBN 0-910311-57-9 $8.99

The Devil's Web
by Pat Pulling with Kathy Cawthon

This explosive exposé presents the first comprehensive guide to childhood and adolescent occult involvement. Written by a nationally recognized occult crime expert, the author explains how the violent occult underworld operates and how they stalk and recruit our children, teen-agers, and young adults for their evil purposes.

ISBN Trade Paper 0-910311-59-5 $8.99
ISBN Hardcover 0-910311-63-3 $16.99

Dinosaurs and the Bible
by David W. Unfred

Every reader, young and old, will be fascinated by this ever-mysterious topic—exactly what happened to the dinosaurs? Author David Unfred draws a very descriptive picture of the history and fate of the dinosaurs, using the Bible as a reference guide. Did dinosaurs really exist? Does the Bible mention dinosaurs? What happened to dinosaurs, or are there some still living awaiting discovery?

ISBN Hardcover 0-910311-70-6 $12.99

God's Rebels
by Henry Lee Curry III

From his unique perspective Dr. Henry Lee Curry III offers a fascinating look at the lives of some of our greatest Southern religious leaders during the Civil War. The rampant Evangelical Christianity prominent at the outbreak of the Civil War, asserts Dr. Curry, is directly traceable to the 2nd Great Awakening of the early 1800s. The evangelical tradition, with its emphasis on strict morality, individual salvation, and emotional worship, had influenced most of Southern Protestantism by this time. Southerners unquestionably believed the voice of the ministers to be the "voice of God"; consequently, the church became one of the most powerful forces influencing Confederate life and morale. Inclined toward a Calvinistic emphasis on predestination, the South was confident that God would sustain its way of life.

ISBN: Trade Paper 0-910311-67-6 $12.99
ISBN: Hardcover 0-910311-68-4 $21.99

Hidden Dangers of the Rainbow
by Constance Cumbey

The first book to uncover and expose the New Age movement, this national #1 best-seller paved the way for all other books on the subject. It has become a giant in its category. This book provides the vivid expose of the New Age movement, which the author contends is dedicated to wiping out Christianity and establishing a one world order. This movement, a vast network of occult and pagan organizations, meets the tests of prophecy concerning the Antichrist.

ISBN 0-910311-03-X $9.99

Image of the Ages
by Dr. David Webber

Are the secular humanists' plans for a New World Order about to be realized? How will the establishment of this order affects you and your family? David Webber, author of *The Image of the Ash*, explains how modern technology, artificial intelligence, and other scientific advances will be used in the near future to manipulate the masses.

ISBN 0-910311-38-2 $7.99

Last Days Collection
by Last Days Ministries

Heart-stirring, faith challenging messages from Keith Green, David Wilkerson, Melody Green, Leonard Ravenhill, Winkie Pratney, Charles Finney and William Booth are designed to awaken complacent Christians to action.

ISBN 0-961-30020-5 $8.95

Inside the New Age Nightmare
by Randall Baer

Now, for the first time, one of the most powerful and influential leaders of the New Age movement has come out to expose the deceptions of the organizations he once led. New Age magazines and articles for many years hailed Randall Baer as Their most "radically original" and "advanced" thinker . . . "light years ahead of others" says leading New Age magazine *East-West Journal*. His bestselling books on quartz crystals, self-transformation, and planetary ascension have won worldwide acclaim and been extolled by New Agers from all walks of life.

Hear, from a New Age insider, the secret plans they have spawned to take over our public, private, and political institutions. Discover the seduction of the demonic forces at work—turned from darkness to light, Randall Baer reveals the methods of the New Age movement as no one else can. Find out what you can do to stop the New Age movement from destroying our way of life.

ISBN 0-910311-58-7 $8.99

New World Order:
The Ancient Plan of Secret Societies
by William T. Still

For thousands of years, secret societies have cultivated an ancient plan which has powerfully influenced world events. Until now, this secret plan has remained hidden from view. This book presents new evidence that a military take-over of the U.S. was considered by some in the administration of one of our recent presidents. Although averted, the forces behind it remain in secretive positions of power.

ISBN 0-910311-64-1 $8.99

Kinsey, Sex and Fraud: The Indoctrination of a People
by Dr. Judith A. Reisman and Edward Eichel

Kinsey, Sex and Fraud describes the research of Alfred Kinsey which shaped Western society's beliefs and understanding of the nature of human sexuality. His unchallenged conclusions are taught at every level of education—elementary, high school and college—and quoted in textbooks as undisputed truth.

The authors clearly demonstrate that Kinsey's research involved illegal experimentations on several hundred children. The survey was carried out on a non-representative group of Americans, including disproportionately large numbers of sex offenders, prostitutes, prison inmates and exhibitionists.

ISBN Hardcover 0-910311-20-X $19.99

Psychic Phenomena Unveiled: Confessions of a New Age Warlock
by John Anderson

He walked on hot coals and stopped his heart. As one of Los Angeles' most recognized psychics, John Anderson was on top of the world. His ability to perform psychic phenomena converted the most stubborn unbeliever into a true believer in occult power. But John Anderson sensed his involvement in the occult was destroying him. This book was written to expose the trickery behind the New Age magic and address man's attraction to the occult.

ISBN 0-910311-49-8 $8.99

Seduction of the Innocent Revisited
by John Fulce

If you haven't picked up a comic book in a few years, you're in for a real shock! Today's comics are filled with obscene images, occult symbols and even nudity. There are no more heroes battling the forces of evil. A constant anti-Christian theme similar to the anti-Semitic theme found in German literature during the 1920s and 30s should alarm even the casual observer.

ISBN 0-910311-66-8 $8.99

"Soft Porn" Plays Hardball
by Dr. Judith A. Reisman

With amazing clarity, the author demonstrates that pornography imposes on society a view of women and children that encourages violence and sexual abuse. As crimes against women and children increase to alarming proportions, it's of paramount importance that we recognize the cause of this violence. Pornography should be held accountable for the havoc it has wreaked in our homes and our country.

ISBN Trade Paper 0-910311-65-X $8.99
ISBN Hardcover 0-910311-92-7 $16.95

Teens and Devil Worship
by Charles Evans

Charles Evans was a teen-age Satanist, introduced to the occult through his obsession with heavy metal music. "I noticed that all of my favorite performers promoted occult or satanic practices in their songs...Soon I had a personal library in the black arts...I easily began leading others into the worship of Satan. Teen-agers would beg to join my coven." His dabbling soon became an addiction. Revealing the whys and hows of teen involvement in Satanism, this book also shows what can be done to prevent involvement.

ISBN 1-56384-004-9 $8.99

_____ America ... 99 _____
_____ Angel V ... 99 _____
_____ Battle P ... 99 _____

_____ Blessing ... 99 _____
_____ Crystal ... 99 _____
_____ Deadly ... 99 _____
_____ The De ... 99 _____
_____ Dinosa ... 99 _____
_____ *Don't ... 99 _____

_____ En Rou ... 99 _____
_____ Exposi ... 99 _____
_____ Face th ... 99 _____
_____ *False ... 99 _____
_____ From F ... 99 _____
_____ *Gays ... 99 _____
_____ Hidde ... 99 _____
_____ *Hitler ... 99 _____
_____ Inside ... 99 _____
_____ *A Jew ... 99 _____
_____ *Journ ... 99 _____
_____ Kinsey ... 99 _____

_____ Last D ... 95 _____
_____ Legen ... 99 _____
_____ New V ... 99 _____
_____ *One ... 99 _____

_____ *Politi ... .99 _____
_____ Psych ... 4.99 _____
_____ * Real ... .99 _____
_____ "Soft ... 5.95 _____
_____ *Subtl ... .99 _____
_____ Teens ... 8.99 _____
_____ To Gr ... set _____
_____ Touch ... 8.99 _____
_____ Troja ... 9.99 _____
_____ Twist ... 9.99 _____
_____ *Whe ... 9.99 _____
with
_____ Who ... 8.99 _____
_____ *You Hit Like a Girl—Elsa Houtz & William J. Ferkile ... 9.99 _____

* *New Title*

Shipping and Handling _____
Total _____

AVAILABLE AT BOOKSTORES EVERYWHERE or order direct from:
Huntington House Publishers • P.O. Box 53788 • Lafayette, LA 70505
Send check/money order. For faster service use VISA/MASTERCARD
call toll-free 1-800-749-4009.
Add: Freight and handling, $3.50 for the first book ordered, and $.50 for each additional
book up to 5 books.

Enclosed is $_____ including postage.
VISA/MASTERCARD#_____ Exp. Date_____
Name_____ Phone: (   )_____
Address_____
City, State, Zip_____